A Good Name

A Good Name

A History of the Nicks Family of
Dickson County, Tennessee

by Tommy Nicks

A Good Name:
A History of the Nicks Family of
Dickson County, Tennessee

© 2017 by Tommy Nicks

ISBN: 978-0-692-94377-9

PO Box 726
Dickson, TN 37056

In memory of my Father

CARNEY B. NICKS

(1915-2003)

and

to my Mother

JANE REEVES NICKS

Contents

List of Illustrations

Acknowledgments

This project would never have become a reality without the love of my life, Judy McCoin Nicks. Her patience and understanding together with her dedication to my desire to do this were never ending. In this book, as in my life, she deserves much credit.

I will always be indebted to my good friend Bard Young for his extraordinary editing abilities, for his willingness to share his talents and most of all for his friendship. He has a unique ability with the written word, and the best of this book belongs to him.

Nancy Nicks Norton would never let this project die. Repeatedly, she told me that these stories had to be committed to writing. I have been blessed by her mutual feelings for our family, by her encouragement and by her eternal dedication to the comma.

Introduction

Some years ago, I determined the importance of committing to writing the information I have acquired regarding our Nicks Family. I wanted to tell the story of our family in a fashion that expressed how they lived and who they really were. Our ancestors were much more than dates in a family tree; they lived full lives, they endured many hardships and some successes, and they played a role in the settlement of the Middle Tennessee frontier. They were key participants in the establishment and growth of whole communities. This is what I wanted to pass on to my children and grandchildren: the story of our family and how they built lives for *their* children and grandchildren. Their values continue to determine who we are today.

I sometimes wished that I could have written several stories at once, presenting them in parallel columns so that the reader could follow all of these stories simultaneously, thereby giving a sense of the way numerous events run side by side in the passage of time. Our ancestors did not live in a void that isolated them from one another or from the events of the day. That, however, could be accomplished only by an accomplished writer, which I am not; so, this may be a difficult read for some. This book is neither a novel nor a biography, but a genealogical document that includes some dates and a lot of family history, but it is also a story, and I have tried to tell that story with as much care and love as I have in me.

The older the ancestor, the less information I had to work with. Many documents have not survived to provide the details of the lives of our early ancestors. Local and regional histories give the most basic of information about their existence prior to arriving in Tennessee; however, this information sometimes fails to present a comprehensive account of our family, broadly speaking. Information regarding our family prior to leaving North Carolina is almost entirely based on land documents and the repetitive use of certain given names over several generations. I have tried to distinguish between those things that I believe to be true and that those things that have been proven. In all cases, I have tried to document my sources.

At the end of the day, this book is really about my grandfather, Buckner Clay Nicks and his wife Katherine Lyle, but begins with our family's migration to America and their later relocation to the Tennessee Wilderness. As the chapters proceed, I follow our linage with the information I have about each family. I have also tried to include information about their world and the events that shaped their lives. I have attempted to lay a foundation of information that will help us understand what shaped the lives of B. C. and Kate.

I have included in the Appendixes some straightforward genealogical information that may help the reader keep up with who is who. Also included in the Appendixes are copies of old correspondence between Kate Nicks and her mother and some letters from Kate to her boys in 1940 that shed light on B.'s illness.

There will be errors and please forgive me when you find them. If they are errors of grammar, I would ask that you correct them and move on. If they are errors of fact, please let me know and I will correct my copy.

Initially, I plan to distribute this book to my children, my grandchildren and my Nicks cousins. If you desire copies for your children and grandchildren, let me know and I can make those available.

A Good Name

Chapter 1

The Buffalo Presbyterian Church

The first Nickses to arrive in America were of the ethnic group that is known as the Scotch-Irish. The information we have regarding our Nicks family in colonial America always places our folks with the Scotch-Irish, both geographically and in their beliefs.

Scotch-Irish Americans are descendants of Presbyterian and other Ulster Protestant Dissenters from various parts of Ireland, but usually from the province of Ulster, who migrated to North America during the 18th and 19th centuries.[1] The term Scotch-Irish is used primarily in the United States, while people in Great Britain or Ireland who are of a similar ancestry identify themselves as Ulster Scots people.[2] Most of these immigrants had come to Ireland from Scotland to seek economic opportunities and freedom from the control of the Scottish Episcopal Church. These included 200,000 Scottish Presbyterians who settled in Ireland from 1608 to 1697. Later, attempts to force the Church of England's control over dissident Protestants in Ireland would lead to further waves of emigration to the American colonies.[3]

Little did they know that their quest for basic human rights would not end with their arrival in the American Colonies. Their frustrations with the English Monarchy would continue for another seventy-five years, after which they would play a large role in liberating an entire continent from British rule. They were instrumental in shaping the destiny of our Nation.[4]

At first, it was anything but easy. Living conditions were crude; the entire country was a wilderness with only a few cleared fields here and there. Their homes were the rudest of cabins, made from logs hand cut from the forest. Floors were of dirt and roofs would have been made of thatch. Most of these dwellings would have only one door and one window. Their food largely would have been the meat of wild animals, and their clothes were made from pelts. Those first years would have been hard.[5]

These trying conditions would last only a few years, for they were an industrious and hard-working people who desired only their freedom to worship and to own land. Many would arrive first in Pennsylvania and Maryland, and it is estimated that between 1740 and 1750 they arrived at the rate of 10,000 per year.[6] Because of the number of immigrants that were arriving, landowners in these colonies often instructed their agents not to sell any land to these newcomers, out of fear that they would soon gain political control.

These Scotch-Irish people were again being obstructed in their efforts to obtain land. Those that had settled in southeastern Pennsylvania and northern Maryland formed the Nottingham Presbyterian Church. They were identified by their adherence to Old-Side Presbyterianism.[7] Under the bounds of this church they formed the Nottingham Colony to seek land in new frontiers for their families.

The Colony sent agents to North Carolina to seek and secure tracts of land that these families could settle on. The lands that would be acquired were located in Guilford County, North Carolina, near the present city of Greensboro. The Nottingham Colony would move their families there around 1852.[8]

One of the families that made this move and purchased land along Buffalo Creek was our ancestor John Nicks Sr. John Sr. was likely the son of George Blake Nicks and Phoebe Price, who had migrated from Ireland and settled in the Talbot County area of Maryland.[9]

John Nicks Sr. is believed to have married Margaret Quinton Edwards, and they would have a daughter named Phoebe and sons named George, John Jr. and Quinton. These names were all derived from court records that have survived in Guilford County. These names also appear in subsequent generations and have become part of the foundation on which we establish our heritage.

Within the first few years after their arrival in Guilford County, North Carolina, this group would establish the Buffalo Presbyterian Church. This congregation remains active today and is located in close proximity to the lands that John Nicks Sr. purchased.

In his book *History of Buffalo Presbyterian Church and Her People*, S. M. Rankin includes the following information regarding John Nicks: "John Nicks secured grants for two sections just east of the church. His wife was Margaret, and their children were Sarah, George (1756–1838), John, Elizabeth Nancy, Quinton and two other daughters. George would live out his life in Guilford County. Quinton and John (Jr.) moved to Tennessee after the Revolutionary War. John Nicks, Sr. died in 1781."[10]

In support of this information, I am in possession of a copy of a land grant to John Nicks Sr. that transfers 650 acres of land on Buffalo Creek. This transfer was made by the Earl of Granville, who controlled these lands through the authority of King George II. This property was located near the Buffalo Presbyterian Church.

In 1902, Sallie W. Stockard wrote a history of the area entitled *The History of Guilford County, North Carolina*. In this publication, she speaks of these pioneers and their arrival to the area. She states that they "came not as adventurers or hunters, not as outlaws and wanderers, but as intelligent men, with good worldly substance, with the needed implements of industry, with civilization and the church. These people were dissenters seeking religious liberty as well as homes for their wives and children." Ms. Stockard also provides insights into the characteristics of these Scotch-Irish people. "They are mainly noticeable in thought-movements. From this stock have come our public men, soldiers, politicians and statesmen. They were Whig in principle. Internal improvements, public education and industrial development are ideas of the Whigs."[11]

In 1741 the Nottingham Presbyterian congregation divided over the subject of revivals. Those who formed the Buffalo congregation were on the conservative side of that argument and did not believe that demonstrations of emotion during worship services were scriptural. This colony had never known anything but hardship and privation. They had come to America that they might have civil and religious liberty, and they were happy in this freedom.[12]

This was the environment that welcomed John Nicks Sr. when he moved to North Carolina, and it was here that he would raise his family. During his lifetime America would gain its independence, and the deciding battle of the Revolutionary War was fought at the Guilford County Courthouse. Major General Nathanial Greene led a force of 4,500 Americans against a 2,100 man British army commanded by General Charles Cornwallis. The colonists prevailed in this battle that many believe to have been the turning point in the Revolutionary War.[13] It has been stated that every man of the Buffalo congregation who was of military age was in the service.[14]

According to S. M. Rankin in his book, *History of Buffalo Presbyterian Church and Her People*, three sons of John Nicks Sr.

6

served in the Revolutionary War; George, John Jr. and Quinton. George received a pension and John Jr. and Quinton later went to that part of Tennessee reserved for North Carolina soldiers.[15] In 1783 the state assembly passed an act reserving for the North Carolina soldiers a certain body of land in the territory of Tennessee. This is the area to where John Jr. would later migrate to in 1800[16.]

John Jr. is believed to have been born in 1753 and may have been married to Margaret Amanda Doak. We know that John Jr. served in the Revolutionary War and was residing in Guilford County, North Carolina, in 1790, as per the census of 1790.

John moved to Hickman County in about 1800. Among his family was a son who was born in North Carolina on March 6, 1794, who was named Absalom Doak Nicks. Their journey would have been a difficult one, especially considering that they traveled with small children.

Many who made this journey would have come by way of the very rugged "roads" that were in existence at the time. The first leg would have been to where Ashville, North Carolina is located today. From there the French Broad Trail would have taken them to Knoxville. The journey from the Knoxville area to Nashville was made on the Nashville Road, which was built in 1788. This wagon road was large enough to accommodate large wagons and led across the Cumberland Plateau west some 180 miles to Nashville. Old U. S. Route 70 followed this passageway. Today much of the old road runs parallel to Interstate 40.[17]

Once in the Nashville area, it is most probable that the last leg of the journey to Hickman County would have been made over the Natchez Trace. A portion of the Natchez Trace runs in close proximity to the Little Lot area where our family would settle. This community lies along the Duck River, between Columbia and Centerville, Tennessee.

Most families who made that journey would have come by wagons that were pulled by horses, mules or oxen. It would have been difficult beyond our imagination. All of their tools, utensils and wagons would have been crude, their food supplies limited, and the travel would have been slow and dangerous. Indians were still a threat to the area. The distance traveled would have been over 500 miles.

To appreciate the difficulties of travel during this period, consider the condition of the Trace at the time of the Nicks migration to Middle Tennessee. The Trace at that time was simply a path that had been the route of migrating buffalos as they sought out grazing lands and salt licks. It was later used by the Indians and then by flatboat traders who had floated from Nashville to New Orleans to deliver goods and would use the Trace as a path back home. Not until the War of 1812 would any federal improvements be provided and only then to accommodate Andrew Jackson's march to New Orleans.

It appears that John Jr. came into possession of his lands through a land grant that was awarded to Revolutionary War veterans in compensation for their service. The State Assembly made these land grants available through an act that reserved these lands in the Tennessee territory. Tennessee was then considered to be on the western frontier and was a part of North Carolina.

While John Jr. received his grant in 1783, the interior of Tennessee did not begin its settlement until about 1800. There were several factors that delayed the development of the interior. First, the issue of which States controlled the western frontier was a contentious one that was not resolved until the original 13 states adopted a constitution on September 17, 1787, over four years after the end of the Revolutionary War. With the passage of the constitution, it was agreed that these lands would belong to the Federal Government and the rules of settlement were established.

Secondly, the Tennessee territory was settled from east to west. Knoxville was founded in 1789 and soon became the center of Tennessee's population. The opening of the Nashville Road from Knoxville to Nashville did not occur until 1795. Prior to the opening of this road, passage by wagon into the interior of the State was almost impossible.

Finally, Tennessee was not admitted to the Union until June 1, 1796. It was after this that the migration into the Middle Tennessee area began to increase. Governments began to be formed, the risk of attacks by Indians became less and trade and activity began to increase.

This is what the records that are available tell us regarding the movement of our early Nicks family to Tennessee. While there is much information that we do not have, what we do have is largely due to the records available through the Buffalo Presbyterian Church. Again, much of our family connections have been made through the interpolation of the available records with our known family relationships. Personally, and based on the historical writings and records in Guilford County, I am most comfortable with the fact that John Jr., the son of John Sr. and grandson of George Blake Nicks, was the father of our direct ancestor, Absalom Doak Nicks.

Chapter 2

Absalom Doak Nicks and Settlement in Tennessee

The earliest ancestor that our Nicks family can claim with absolute certainty is Absalom Doak Nicks. Absalom was born in North Carolina on March 6, 1794. According to the *Goodspeed's Histories,* Absalom and his father came to Hickman County, Tennessee, in 1800.[18] We know that Absalom would have been about 6 years old when his family made the journey from North Carolina to Tennessee—very young boy to have made this difficult journey.

Absalom Nicks was a veteran of the War of 1812. In 1814 he enlisted in the First Regiment, Volunteers, Mounted Gunmen. Company Muster Rolls show that he enlisted on April 28, 1814, and that he served through April 29, 1815. These records also indicate that Absalom was entitled to an allowance for the use of a horse at a rate of 40¢ per day. This information is taken from muster and pay rolls, though those records do not indicate what type of service was performed.

In 1815, Absalom lived on the headwaters of Mill Creek in the 5th Civil District of Hickman County, as did his brother, William Nicks, a preacher.[19] Absalom was engaged in farming and

10

in transporting salt to Salem, Illinois.[20] These two brothers and their distinct vocations in 1815 would have profound implications on how they and their ancestors would make their living.

Beginning around 1800 and during the first half of the 19th century the iron ore industry would have an economic impact on the area in terms of jobs and opportunities. Furnaces and forges were located in several areas of both Dickson and Hickman Counties and were owned by James Robertson, Montgomery Bell, Robert Baxter, Richard Napier and others. This industry had a direct impact on where our ancestors would eventually settle.

Hauling goods in that time required wagons and teams of mules or horses. The delivery of goods produced in an area would require much equipment and many skills, including the maintenance of stock and equipment, the raising of feed and blacksmithing. There were no railroads at this time, and what limited roads existed were primitive and difficult to travel. Men operating these types of operations were then known as teamsters or wagoners.

Being a teamster or wagoner was not an easy job. Consider the trip from Little Lot, Tennessee, to Salem, Illinois, a distance of over 300 miles. The trip would have required more than just the wagons required to transport the goods, but also wagons to carry the food and supplies needed by those making the trip. It was also necessary to carry enough feed for the mules. One of the wagons would have been a forge wagon that carried the items needed to shoe the mules and to make the needed repairs to the wagons.

A few numbers provide a hint of the effort and complexities involved. A caravan of ten wagons would require as many as 60 mules and the harnesses needed to outfit them. The men making the journey would have not only been drivers, but also cooks and blacksmiths. With that many animals to care for, several men would have been required to maintain all those mules and

11

their harnesses. If the teams could cover 15 miles a day, the trip would require 20 days, one way.

Farming was the most common listed profession in the census data of that time and would be for the next 90 years. Blacksmithing was a trade that would be practiced in the families of Absalom's descendants. Teamsters of that time not only hauled goods produced in their communities, but would provide the valuable service of hauling back the needed supplies, seeds, tools and other items necessary for the subsistence of the families in their area. In time, this service would lead many in our family into the merchandising field, both retail and wholesale.

The early Nicks families also were prominent in the preaching of the gospel during the period we now refer to as the Restoration Movement. William Nicks was a brother of Absalom and was a well-known preacher of the gospel. He, and others, would hold revivals at a place called "The Stand" near the community of Shady Grove, Tennessee. The Stand was an area south of Shady Grove and at one time consisted of a small church house and a cemetery. Its proximity to the Natchez Trace made it a popular place for revivals involving various denominations. William Nicks is buried there and his grave and tombstone are well preserved.

The Restoration Movement developed out of the Presbyterian Church under the leadership of Alexander Campbell and Barton Warren Stone. This movement was also known as the Stone-Campbell Movement. The pioneers of this movement were seeking to reform the church from within and sought "the unification of all Christians in a single body patterned after the church of the New Testament."[21] It has been described as the "oldest ecumenical movement in America."[22] Early followers of this movement described themselves as "Christians," "Disciples of Christ" and "Churches of Christ." (An interesting note: Barton Warren Stone attended Guilford Academy in Greensboro, North

Carolina and while studying there became interested in becoming an ordained Presbyterian minister.[23])

This movement would have a deep influence upon Absalom Doak Nicks and his family. William Nicks's son, John, would become known as Elder John Nicks and was one of the founders of the Centerville Church of Christ in 1879. Absalom Doak Nicks Jr. would become a Church of Christ preacher, his occupation listed as minister in the 1900 census. Others would be named for leaders in this movement. Absalom Sr. would name his fourth son, and our direct ancestor, Barton Warren Stone Nicks, after the well-known Restoration preacher of the same name. Absalom's oldest son, Perry, would name a son after Tolbert Fanning, another well-known gospel preacher and co-founder of the *Gospel Advocate* along with David Lipscomb. Barton Warren Stone Nicks would donate land in Stayton, Tennessee, for the building of the Friendship Church of Christ. He would also agree to adopt a young man in 1884, William Thomas Deloach, who would be the grandfather of Clarence Deloach, a well-known Church of Christ preacher who was raised in Dickson County and spent over 10 years as the minister of the Walnut Street congregation in Dickson, Tennessee.

Our family history in Tennessee had commenced. The events of these early years had laid the foundation for a set of values and beliefs that would shape our family for generations to come.

Chapter 3
Absalom Doak Nicks and the Establishment of a Tennessee Family

Absalom Nicks (1794–1848) married Hester Perry (1788–1858) in about 1815. The exact date is unknown; however, we know that he was involved in the War of 1812 until April of 1815, and we know that their first child was born on December 2, 1816.

Between 1816 and 1832 twelve children would be born to this marriage. The compilation of whole families prior to 1850 is a challenge. Prior to 1850, census records listed only the head of the household and then tallied the number of males and females in the house by various age groups.

My records include those individuals listed as the children of Absalom in a genealogical collection compiled by Ruth Hunt in the early 1980s. Some of this information I have verified through later census records, wills, death certificates and marriage records, but some have not been validated. I have not deleted any of the individuals listed by Ms. Hunt since I have found no conflicting data.

What follows is information I have found that would be of interest regarding Absalom's children. As you will see, we have no material on some of them. I have left out the information on

14

Barton Warren Stone Nicks because we have descended from his line, and he will be discussed in a later chapter.

The first-born child of Absalom and Hester was Perry Nicks, who was born on December 2, 1816, in Hickman County. He died in 1863. He married Rebecca Davis in 1838 in Hickman County Tennessee. She was born in 1824 in North Carolina and died in 1870. To this marriage were born 8 children. Most of the Dickson County Nickses who are not in our direct line descend from Perry Nicks, most particularly from his son Tolbert Fanning Nicks. Some of these "cousins" would be Bob Wolcott, Walter Nicks, Bobby Speight, Steve Deloach, Glenn Hicks, Bill Stewart and Harriet Walker Hinkle. Many of these Nickses were born and raised in the Jones Creek area between Dickson and White Bluff. The Tolbert Fanning Nicks farmhouse is located on Southerland Road where Larry Joe Scott and his wife now reside. Tolbert Fanning Nicks was a church of Christ preacher and was named for Tolbert Fanning who was a renowned preacher of the gospel. Many members of this family are buried at the Rock Church of Christ cemetery in Dickson, Tennessee.

Two years later in 1818 a second son, named Quinton was born in Hickman County. He would pass away on August 14, 1884, in Arkansas City, Arkansas. He married Elizabeth Walker. She was born in 1821 in Tennessee and died in 1880. At some point prior to 1847, Quinton moved to Old River, Arkansas, with his father, Absalom.

Their third child was a daughter named Mary who was born in 1820. Little information exists on Mary, but according to Ruth Hunt's research she is believed to have died in 1897.

On December 9, 1821, another son named Allen Perry Nicks would be born to this marriage. He died on April 16, 1910, in Nashville, Davidson County, Tennessee. He was married to Susan Rosanne Blocker on September 26, 1841, in Maury County. She was born on June 5, 1824, in Maury County. She died on

October 23, 1871, in Bon Aqua, Tennessee. Allen Peery Nicks assisted in the construction of the Rock Church of Christ between Dickson and White Bluff. Most of his life was lived in the area of Jones Creek/White Bluff, Tennessee.

According to the record in Ruth Hunt's compilation, the fifth child born to this marriage was born in about 1823, her name and death date unknown. This lack of information would lead us to believe that she could have died as an infant.

Barton Warren Stone Nicks, our direct ancestor, was the sixth child and fourth son born to Absalom and Hester. He was born on July 24, 1824, in Hickman County, and died on April 8, 1894, in Stayton, Tennessee. He married America Agnes McGraw, daughter of Caleb McGraw and Mary Nichols, on June 14, 1847. America was born on October 6, 1831, in Hickman County. She died on March 19, 1905, in Stayton.

John H. Nicks was born about 1825 and died in 1893. According to census records, he was living with his brother, B. W. S. Nicks in 1850, and his profession was listed as a wagoner. In 1880, he was living with another brother, Isaac, in Montgomery County, as a widower with three small children. His occupation at that time was listed as a farm laborer.

The eighth child born into this family was also a son, Absalom Doak Nicks Jr., who was born on July 19, 1826, in Mill Creek, Hickman County, Tennessee. He died on January 24, 1904, and is buried in Scotts Graveyard, Cheatham County, Tennessee. He married Margaret Sophie Blocker on June 15, 1845, in Maury County, Tennessee. She was born on July 10, 1829, in Williamsport, Maury County, Tennessee. She died on January 9, 1918, in Hickman County.

Some sources state that Absalom Jr. was a blacksmith by trade, but he is listed in the census records of 1880 and 1900 as a minister. He was loyal to the United States during the civil war. After the war ended, the state government was appointed by the

16

federal government. Absalom Jr. was appointed by the Andrew Johnson administration as the state representative from his district. When he refused to go along with a proposition that would only allow voting rights to those known to be loyal to the U.S. during the war, he was replaced. Later, when the right to vote was restored, he ran for the same office and was elected. In the 1870 census his profession is listed as legislator and he was living in the 12th district of Dickson County.

Isaac H. Nicks the ninth child was born on October 6, 1827. He died in 1898. His wife's name is listed as Charlotte in the census records. In the 1850 census, he was also living in Montgomery County with his brother, B. W. S. Nicks. According to the 1870 census, he had remained in Montgomery County and his occupation was listed as a miner. In 1880 he was again in Montgomery County, where he was listed as a farmer. In 1880 his older brother, John H., was a widower and listed in the household. Isaac was buried in the Lone Oak Cemetery in Montgomery County. He was known by the name Ike.

Another unknown daughter was born in 1829. Again, there are no known records regarding this child, the reason may well being infant death.

Robert Anderson Nicks was born in May of 1830. He died in 1909. He first married Cassandra Rawlson in 1855 and later married Nancy Ann Puckett. In the 1850 census he too was living with his older brother, B. W. S. Nicks. This would make three siblings living with our ancestor in the 1850 census, most likely owing to their occupations as wagoners and blacksmiths. It appears that Robert moved to Texas and served the Confederacy there during the Civil War. In 1900 he was living in Red River, Texas. He died and was buried in Paden, Okfuskee County, Oklahoma in 1909.

The last child born to Absalom and Hester was Stephen P. Nicks, who was born on February 15, 1832. In 1850 Stephen was

17

living with his mother, Hester, and her servant Phoebe, a black female 64 years old. In this census record, he is listed as 18 years old. To date, I have not found any trace of him after 1850.

Between 1816 and 1832, a period of 16 years, twelve children were born to Absalom and Hester, 9 boys and 3 girls. All of the children with the exception of the two unknown daughters lived to see adulthood. Absalom would have been 22 years of age at the birth of the first child, and Hester would have been 28. At the birth of their last child, he would have been 38 years old, and she would have been 44.

Sometime in the 1840s, Absalom moved to Arkansas County, Arkansas, and died there on July 14, 1848. He died without writing a will. His second child, Quinton, had also moved there and was named by the courts to settle Absalom's affairs. Absalom was buried in Arkansas County, but the exact location is unknown.

Barton Warren Stone Nicks was married on June 14, 1847. He had left his parents' home in 1846 when he was 22 years old.[24] Barton may have been living in Montgomery County, Tennessee, at the time of his father's death.

Any explanation as to why Absalom moved is only speculation. There are no records of a divorce or family problems. Quinton remained in Arkansas after his father's death, and subsequent census records indicate that he lived in Arkansas City, a delta-type region close to the Mississippi River. The most likely explanation for the move is that it was simply an effort to find to a more fertile area. Absalom's family had moved west at the beginning of the century. Many who made the initial move continued to move west as the century progressed, seeking opportunities to improve their circumstances.

These census facts of 1850 provide us with much interesting information regarding our family. We find Absalom's widow, Hester, living in Hickman County with her 18-year-old son, Stephen P., and a 64-year-old female black servant, named Phoebe.

Stephen's occupation is listed as a farmer. Next door to Hester lived her oldest son, Perry and his wife and 6 children (5 boys and 1 girl), ages 1 to 10 years. It is obvious that Perry did not make the trip to Arkansas. Two doors down from Hester lived her brother-in-law, William Nicks (the preacher) with his wife, Sara Sally, and their 7 children, ages 14–36 (5 boys and 2 girls). In William's household at that time was the oldest son, John, who would become known as Elder John Nicks, who helped establish the Centerville Church of Christ.

Hester Perry Nicks would die in July of 1858 and is buried in Williamsport, Tennessee. The exact place of her burial is not known.

It is interesting to note that John Nicks Jr., who we believe was the father of Absalom, had both a sister and a grandmother named Phoebe. Also, it was not uncommon for slaves to be named for relatives or members of the family. Absalom's great-aunt Phoebe born in 1738; the slave Phoebe would have been born in 1786. Absalom's father also had a son named Quinton. The circumstantial evidence that John Nicks Jr. was Absalom's father is substantial.

As discussed earlier, the 1850 census lists Barton Warren Stone Nicks and his wife living in Montgomery County with 3 of his brothers: John H., age 25, Isaac H., age 23, and Robert Anderson, age 20. Barton would have been 26 years old. Barton listed his occupation as a blacksmith while the others are listed as wagoners. The family had dispersed during the 1840s. That same census (1850) gives some indication of the state's population's growth rate, which had swelled from 250,000 in 1809 to over 1 million in 1850.

The following timeline forms a perspective on the events that had occurred during Absalom's life in Tennessee.

1801 – Thomas Jefferson is President and the purchase of the Louisiana territory was made.

1805 – The Lewis and Clark Expedition takes place.

1812 – President James Madison declares war on England.

1820 – The population of the U.S. is 9,638,453, with 1,538,022 of those being slaves.

1829 – Andrew Jackson is elected President.

1830 – The Indian Removal Act leads to the Trail of Tears.

1837 – The Panic of 1837 begins, brought on by Jackson's bank laws.

1845 – Texas becomes a State.

1846 – James K. Polk is elected President. His home is located in Columbia, Tennessee, about 25 miles from our Absalom.

1849 – Zachary Taylor becomes President.

Inventions developed during this period point to how primitive life was on the frontier when Absalom moved to Tennessee. They include the steam locomotive, the tin can, matches, the first typewriter, the reaper, the wrench, the first revolver, the telegraph, a bicycle, the sewing machine and the safety pin. Yet, in 1850, there was no electricity, no plumbing and no telephone or railways in the Tennessee area. There was no refrigeration, pasteurization or ice. Most everything we enjoy and take for granted in the way of conveniences did not exist.

Up until 1850, Hickman County and Middle Tennessee were referred to as the Western Frontier, and those that lived there were referred to as settlers. All of the U.S. presidents until this time were either slave owners or under the political influence of the proposition of slavery. Industrialization had not begun, and even though the South maintained control over national policy, much debate had begun over federal control of the states, particularly between the Free states and the Slave states. Much would change in the next 20 years, as civil war would erupt over the issues of federal or state control.

Chapter 4
Barton Warren Stone Nicks, Stayton Settler

Barton Warren Stone Nicks was born on July 24, 1824, and married America Agnes McGraw on June 14, 1847. She was the daughter of Caleb McGraw and was born on October 6, 1831. Barton Warren Stone Nicks would be known throughout his life by either his initials (B.W.S.) or simply as Bart.

The B. W. S. Nicks family Bible records this marriage and states that B. W. S. Nicks resided in Maury County at the time of the marriage and that America lived in Hickman County. The marriage was performed by William Nicks, "a preacher of the Christian Church." This would have been Bart's uncle, a brother to Absalom. The certificate also specifies that they were married in the home of America's father, Caleb McGraw. It also bears the name of a witness, John Nicks. (The Nicks Family Bible is in the possession of Sammy Nicks.) Because John Nicks Jr., the father of Absalom, died in about 1825, this John appears to be a brother or nephew of Absalom. Absalom had moved to Arkansas by this time and was not present for the wedding.[25]

Bart Warren Stone Nicks and America Agnes McGraw

B. W. S. Nicks had remained with his parents until he was 22 years of age.[26] This would suggest that his parents were still in Hickman County in 1846 and did not move to Arkansas until later. For the first year after he left his parents, B.W.S engaged in the manufacture of poplar shingles and, after that, began transporting dry goods, groceries and cotton to Columbia and Williamsport.[27]

He then went to Montgomery County and entered the employ of Robert Baxter at the furnaces and forges.[28] The 1850 census shows Bart living in Montgomery County with his wife, America, his daughter and first child, Mary R. and 3 of his brothers, Isaac Nicks, Robert Anderson Nicks and John H. Nicks. Bart's profession was listed as a blacksmith, while all 3 brothers were listed as wagoners. Next door to Bart in the 1850 census lived another brother, Absalom Doak Nicks Jr., and his wife Margaret. Absalom Jr.'s profession was listed as blacksmith. It would be later that he became a minister and the state representative for Dickson County.

After working in Montgomery County for four years, Bart would return to Williamsport and again engage in teaming and farming. He then went to Laurel Furnace in Dickson County and hauled pig iron to Nashville for about 3 years.[29]

According to a newspaper article written by Earl Schmittou Jr. in 1972 for the *Dickson Free Press*, Bart Nicks first built a small log cabin near a spring about 200 yards northeast of what would later become the Earl Schmittou home.[30] A few years later, he built his permanent home on the site that would later become the Schmittou home. The United States tax assessment list of 1862 shows B. W. S. Nicks as owning 724 acres in the 8th Civil District of Dickson County (Stayton). Schmittou also stated that Bart Nicks and his wife, America Agnes, and their children were some of the earliest settlers of the Stayton, Tennessee, area and were responsible for much of the early pioneer life in Stayton.[31]

The 1850 Slave Census indicates that Bart owned four slaves. All were male, ages 30, 27, 25 and 22. Three of them were listed as "black" and one as "mulatto." That Bart owned slaves at this point in his life provokes some interesting observations. First, slaves were very valuable property in terms of a person's financial worth. Slaves were considered more valuable than real property, especially young males capable of hard labor. Second, there seems to be no correlation between the ownership of another human

24

being and the owner's religious beliefs. Third, slavery had become a very hot and contentious subject of National debate in 1850 between the Slave states and the Free states, and would lead to the secession of southern states in the 1860s and eventually to the Civil War, a war that Bart would neither participate in nor support.

In the mid 1850s, Bart Nicks and his brother, Allen Perry Nicks, would be partners in a hauling business in Dickson County, Tennessee. On January 9, 1855, Allen and Bart entered into an agreement with all of their creditors that placed a mortgage on everything they owned to secure their indebtedness to their creditors. Very few families are fortunate enough to possess this much personal information about an ancestor as early as 1855. The document lists every item of value that the brothers owned, and it contains a complete list of their creditor's names, the county in which the creditor lived, the amounts owed and the due dates of the notes.

The purpose of the mortgage was to secure old debts and to gain access to new funds that would finance another year's operation. The document states that the two brothers intended to carry on the business of "hauling or wagoning" under the name and style of A. P. & B. W. S. Nicks in the year 1855 on behalf of W. C. Napier and for Napier, Holt & Co. The list of property mortgaged is detailed and does not distinguish which brother was the owner of which piece. Some of the items necessary for operation of the business were obviously owned jointly. Some of the personal items are listed in pairs.

The note contains the following assets that were mortgaged. "Items needed to carry on the trade and feed the stock and men include: 56 grown work mules and 10 wagons and the harness for 6 mules to a wagon; 500 barrels of corn, most of which was already in the cribs; 4 tons of hay, 4 cows and calves and 30 head of stock hogs, 200 pounds of lard and 4,000 pounds of pork."

The number of mules used in this operation is an indication of how large a business they operated. The job of feeding and caring for 56 animals would have required the services of several men. Ten wagons would require ten drivers if all the wagons were employed at one time.

Personal items that were listed were: "1 buggy and harness, 6 feather beds, bedsteads and furniture, 2 bureaus, 2 presses, 4 looking glasses, 2 dining tables, 2 dressing tables, 1 dozen chairs, 2 clocks (for time), 2 candle stands, 1 sugar chest, 2 carpets, 1 lounge, 2 saddles, 4 pair of andirons and 2 cradles."

This list of personal items affords us evidence of their prosperity in 1855. The ownership of a sugar chest is particularly significant because only a few families of substance were known to own a sugar chest—the reason being that sugar was considered so valuable that a special piece of furniture was used to store and protect the valuable commodity. They were most often made of cherry and were a furniture item known almost exclusively to Middle Tennessee.

Tools listed in the document included one set of blacksmith tools, six ploughs, hoes, mattocks and axes.

This mortgage also provides information regarding the ownership of slaves by the brothers. A negro man slave named Charles who was about 45 years old was mortgaged. Additionally, the brothers offered as collateral their rights to 1 year's service of six negro men slaves named Tom, Simpson, Sol, Daniel, Carroll and Dick. Also mentioned is 1 year's service of a negro woman named Milly.

Finally, the brothers also mortgaged 25 acres of land in the fourth Civil District of Dickson County (this is in the Montgomery Bell State Park area) that bordered the land of White Bluff Forge & Laurel Furnace.

I have found no evidence that the debt was not paid or how it was paid. On July 26, 1856, approximately 18 months after the execution of the mortgage, B. W. S. Nicks sold "a man slave of black complexion named Charlie" to Leonard Burnett for the sum of $450. One can assume that the mortgage was satisfied because the named slave could not have been sold if he were still mortgaged property.

The business did not continue as a partnership, and according to the 1860 census B.W.S was then employed at the Cumberland Furnace as manager. The term "manager" in this census does not reflect that he was responsible for the overall operation of the Furnace but was used as a general job description. Later information would describe his position there as "coal manager"[32] and the 1880 census lists his occupation as coaler.

The closing of the 1850s and the arrival of the 1860s would bring civil war to reality across the nation, and no family would go untouched. I remember my grandmother, Kate Nicks, relating to me, at an early age, that our Nicks family did
not support the dissolution of the Union and did not participate in the war for either side.

The history books of my school years always presented the war as a conflict between those who owned slaves and those who favored abolition. Movies and books, both historical in nature and fictional, always portrayed the "southerners" as marching off to war to the cheers and well wishes of wives, girlfriends and other supporters, whereas the North was portrayed as those who would destroy a rural way of life that was dependent upon slave labor. While all of that may be true, the issues that drove men to try to dissolve our Union or to die preserving it were much more complicated than a simple division of North vs. South over the slave issue.

Having a limited education in American History and being told at an early age that our "folks" supported the North, you can imagine my surprise when I discovered much later in life that members of our Nicks family were slaveholders—not large, plantation type slave holders, but owners of other human beings nonetheless.

Others of our family also owned slaves. Bart's uncle, William Nicks, who was a preacher in the Christian Church and took part in the great Restoration Movement, was a slave owner. Bart's mother, Hester Perry Nicks, owned a 64-year-old black woman named Phoebe. Allen Perry Nicks, Bart's brother, was a slave owner, as was another brother; Absalom Doak Nicks Jr. Absalom Jr. would serve as a state legislator on the Union ticket and he opposed the war.

I have come to believe that the issues that defined a person's position during this period were more complicated than just the slave question. I believe their conviction with respect to the Civil War was formed by their political, religious and economic experiences. The issues that formed our family's position in this matter were no different from those of other families all over the South, especially in the Border States.

One of the significant "hints" that we can gather from our family history with regard to their political beliefs comes from Bart and America naming their first-born son after Henry Clay. Henry Clay (April 12, 1777—June 29, 1852) was an American lawyer, politician, and skilled orator who represented Kentucky in both the United States Senate and House of Representatives. He served three different terms as Speaker of the House of Representatives and was secretary of state from 1825 to 1829. Clay lost campaigns for President in 1824, 1832 and 1844. Henry Clay was of the Whig Party. While a Congressman and Senator from the State of Kentucky, Henry Clay was a dominant figure in American politics for over forty years. He cost Andrew Jackson his first run for the presidency by backing John Quincy Adams in what has been termed the "corrupt bargain." After the election of Andrew Jackson in 1928, Clay led the opposition to Jackson's policies. He ran against Jackson in 1832 and lost and was defeated again in 1844 as the candidate of the Whig Party when he ran against James K. Polk. Clay was the foremost proponent of the American System, fighting for an increase in tariffs to foster industry in the United States, the use of federal funding to build and maintain infrastructure, and a strong national bank. Dubbed the "Great Pacificator," Clay brokered important compromises during the Nullification Crisis and on the slavery issue. He was instrumental in formulating the Missouri Compromise of 1820 and the Compromise of 1850. He was viewed as the primary representative of Western interests in American politics and was given the name "Henry of the West". A plantation owner, Clay held slaves during his lifetime but freed them in his will.[33]

The Whig Party was a political party active in the middle of the 19th century and was formed in opposition to the policies of President Andrew Jackson and his Democratic Party. This party took their name from those who were in favor of American independence from England. In particular, the Whigs supported the supremacy of Congress over the Presidency and favored a program of modernization and economic protectionism. The party was ultimately destroyed by the question over whether to allow the expansion of slavery to the territories. By the 1856 presidential election, the party was defunct. In the South, the party vanished, but Whig ideology as a policy orientation persisted for decades and played a major role in shaping the modernizing policies of the state governments during Reconstruction.[34]

Twenty-three months after Senator Henry Clay's death, Bart and America named their first-born son after Henry Clay. It speaks volumes about their political beliefs. They would not have been supporters of Andrew Jackson nor of James K. Polk, who was Jackson's handpicked candidate for President. They would have been supporters of a strong central government and in favor of federal funding to build better roads. Remember, Bart and many of his brothers had once been teamsters, and their belief in government investment in infrastructure dates back to their Scotch-Irish heritage.

Consider also that Henry Clay favored a strong national banking system while Jackson did not. It should be remembered that during this time there were no banks, as we know them today, especially in the rural areas of the South. As can be seen in the mortgage agreement discussed earlier, the availability of capital for the operation of a business was a makeshift transaction at best, wherein individuals loaned necessary funds to those who did not have them. Often these individual lenders would loan the funds because their businesses were dependent on the services offered by those who needed the capital.

Clay's third characteristic that helps us understand the views that Bart Nicks might have held was the notion of compromise. There were many in the South who believed the answer to slavery lay in a compromise and not secession. This was particularly true in the Border States, where the economic dependence on slaves was not as critical as on the plantations of the Deep South.

From these bits of information about Senator Henry Clay and his Whig party, we can assume that Barton Warren Stone Nicks was a man who believed in a strong central Government that would provide for economic improvements through federal programs. He likely believed that the slavery question would have been solved best through some type of compromise between North and South—allowing the existence of slavery but limiting expansion.

Also influential on Bart's views regarding civil war would have been his religious beliefs. As discussed earlier, most of the family was involved in the Restoration Movement in Middle Tennessee and the Christian Church.

The Gospel Advocate Company was founded in 1855 by Tolbert Fanning and David Lipscomb. Bart Nicks had a nephew named after Tolbert Fanning. The Christian Church through the publication of the *Gospel Advocate* expressed its strong feelings on the Civil War and how the brethren should respond to it. The following is an excerpt from an article written by Tolbert Fanning and published in the February 1861 edition of the *Gospel Advocate* and was provided to me by Neil W. Anderson, the former publisher of the *Gospel Advocate:*

> Has Christianity changed? Does the Lord still reign over his people? How then can Christians, north or south, east or west, engage in war, even against their brethren, without a full sacrifice of every principle of the Christian institution? How dare the brethren—the preachers—bring themselves to the fearful conclusion, to plunge their swords into the hearts of their brethren? We enter not into the question of right or wrong, in the present controversy. So far as our present object is concerned, we are not interested either way. Our purpose is to labor to satisfy Christians that they are not to settle controversies by the sword. The world is to be conquered and saved by argument, by love divine.[35]

Later in the article, Fanning addresses the issue of slavery and how the Christian might address the problem. This paragraph provides great insight into the moral views held by many Christians who owned slaves:

> We do not deny that the controversy between the North and South is of an exclusively religious character. Be it so. We as Christians should labor to adjust difficulties by peaceable means. Indeed, we are permitted to employ no weapon but the sword of the Spirit, — the Jerusalem blade. True, extreme men in the North say that holding Africans in slavery "is a damnable sin *per se*." What shall we do? Meet the question like men and Christians. Let us hear their strongest arguments, and if we are

31

committing sins so heinous as to shut us out of the eternal mansions, let us confess and forsake our evil deeds. But if it should appear upon examination, that while we have suffered greatly on account of the slavery that has been entailed upon us by Europe and the North, we have done more in the last eighty years to humanize, civilize, and Christianize the negro race, and enlighten benighted Africa than all the world besides, has done to in thousands of years, let the facts be set forth, and let the world see our true position. The storm has been raised mainly by preachers, and it must be quieted by the minister of God. Mere politicians cannot accomplish the work."[36]

The dilemma of owning slaves cannot be better expressed than "what would you have us do?" Thomas Jefferson likened slavery to holding a wolf by the ears: "We can neither hold him, nor safely let him go." James Madison and Henry Clay had also expressed this feeling toward a system that they knew was unsustainable but could not find an acceptable way to end it. I have found no records to date that point to slave ownership by Bart Nicks after he sold a negro man named Charlie for $450 in 1856.

In any case, the instructions and beliefs of the men who led the church with which Bart was affiliated left no doubt about what a follower was expected to do about taking up arms against a brother. It is my belief that many different factors, political, economic and religious, would have shaped Bart's belief in the Union, but none greater than the religious one.

Although the family did not join either side in the "taking up of arms," they would not escape the costs of war. America Agnes's father was Caleb McGraw (in some historical accounts he is referred to as Dr. McGraw), and he resided in the Duck River area of Little Lot, Tennessee. Bart and America were married in his home.

Caleb McGraw was known as a strong Union Man in Hickman County. On June 8, 1861, an election was held before the people to ratify the State Legislature's decision to break away from the Union and join the Confederacy. In Hickman County, this action by the legislature was approved by a vote of 1,400 to 3. One of the three voting against succession was Caleb McGraw, another was his son-in-law, John Baker.[37]

In 1862, on the far side of Anderson's Bend and opposite the mouth of Short Creek, which runs into the Duck River between the mouths of Leatherwood and Lick Creeks, Caleb McGraw was drowned by unknown parties. He was a Federal sympathizer, and it was alleged that he had reported to the Federals the presence of Confederate soldiers at home on furloughs. He was taken, apparently by vigilantes, to the river and told to choose between drowning and taking the oath of allegiance to the Confederate States of America. He refused to take the oath. A rock was tied around his neck, and he was carried in a canoe to the middle of the river. He was again told to choose and he replied, "Drown and be damned!" He was drowned.[38]

In an interview published by the Maury County Historical Society in 1969, W. H. McCaleb of Hickman County provided additional information regarding Caleb McGraw's death. Mr. McCaleb stated that McGraw was a Union man and lived on the ridge road about 10 miles from Centerville at the McGraw ford in Greenfield Bend. Mr. McCaleb further stated that Bart Nicks and John Baker were Caleb's sons-in-law. John Baker would later become the sheriff of Hickman County.[39]

Bushwhackers were unofficial groups of men who were sympathetic to the Confederacy, though not officially affiliated with the military. They were independent bands of men who would roam their home area and raid groups of Union soldiers or local citizens who were known to be Union sympathizers. Jayhawkers were the same, but were of Union support. Hickman County was notorious for the activities of these independent groups during the Civil War and they were involved in more fighting and destruction than the regular armies.

Frank H. Smith's *History of Maury County, Tennessee*, compiled by Maury County Historical Society in 1969 includes the following account of Caleb's murder:

> Ben and Bill Chamberlain were brothers (either Confederate scouts or bushwhackers) and they caught Caleb McGraw hiding on Hen Island awaiting the return of a Federal scouting party. Hal Ray and Dick Ray usually ran with the Chamberlain brothers. McGraw's purpose was to report the recent activity of Confederate soldiers who were home on leave. Two weeks later while fishing, Bill Anderson found McGraw's body much disfigured, fish had eaten his face. Dr. McGraw is buried on the opposite bluff along the river.[40]

An article published on January 7, 1870, the *Columbia Herald* reported on the killing of Hal Ray. The account of Ray's death included the following: "Hal Ray, we learn, was tried for the murder of old man McGraw in Duck River during the War and was acquitted."

Absalom Doak Nicks Jr. (A. D. Nicks) was a brother to Barton Warren Stone Nicks and was a loyal Unionist. Early in his career he was listed as a blacksmith and in 1900 as a Minister. A. D. Nicks was appointed to the State House of Representatives representing Dickson County by Governor Brownlow. This legislature was made up of appointments of loyal Union men and has no number in the series of our State's assemblies. This legislature was known as the "Brownlow Legislature".

Nicks first met with the legislature on April 3, 1865, but later resigned his position prior to the expiration of his term because he did not approve of the bitterly partisan acts of his

34

radical Republican associates. One of the acts that he bitterly opposed was the limiting of the right to vote to unconditional Union men and soldiers of the Union Army.[41] When the right to vote was restored to the people in 1869, A. D. Nicks was elected by the people to the state representative's seat from Dickson County.[42]

We have no record that would provide us with information regarding the specific activities of our Nicks family during the Civil War. What is discussed previously is well documented. We do know that the decade of 1860 was a hard one on all of those who lived in the South. Our family would not have been an exception. The War brought economic havoc to the entire area. We know through census data that in 1860 Bart was an employee of the Cumberland Furnace. After the fall of Fort Donelson in 1862, the Furnace ceased operations for the duration of the war[43]. In 1870 Absalom was again working at the Furnace as the Coal Manager.

All 10 of Bart and America Agnes's children were born between 1848 and 1867. Eight of them would survive their infancy. Our ancestor, Henry Clay Nicks, was the oldest boy. He would have been 7 years old when the Civil War began and 11 when it ended. He would have had memories.

Four of their children would be born in the 1860s, but only 2 would survive. Elenora W. was born on December 24, 1861, but would die on May 4, 1864. Barton Warren Stone Nicks Jr. (Warren) would be born on June 25, 1863. Florence A. Nicks would be born on September 28, 1865, and their last child, Stephen Ulisus, would be born on December 10, 1867. He would die on January 7, 1869.

During the 1860s, Bart and America would not only add children to their own family but would experience the marriage of their oldest two children and the birth of their first grandchildren.

Martha, the second child of Bart and America, would marry Benjamin T. McCaslin on December 20, 1866. Interestingly, Benjamin was a Confederate veteran. The McCaslin's first child,

35

Mary Elizabeth, would be born November 24, 1867. Their second child, Lilburn, would be born on November 13, 1869. The oldest child of Bart and America, Mary R., would marry John J. Hudgins on March 2, 1869. Their first child, Albert E., would be born on November 28, 1869.

A time line relating to the family events of B.W.S. and America gives us a sense of the joy and grief that this family experienced during the 1860s, a period of Civil War in the United States.

12/24/1861 Elenora W. Nicks, their 7th child is born.

2/16/1862 After the fall of Fort Donelson, Cumberland Furnace ceases operations.

8/1/1862 Caleb McGraw, America's father, is killed by bushwhackers.

6/25/1863 Barton Warren Stone Nicks Jr., their 8th child is born.

5/4/1864 Elenora W. Nicks, their 7th child dies.

9/28/1865 Florence A. Nicks, their 9th child is born.

12/20/1866 Martha E. Nicks, their 2d child marries Benjamin T. McCaslin.

11/24/1867 Mary E. McCaslin is born, Bart and America's 1st grandchild.

12/1/1867 Stephen Ulisus Nicks, their 10th and last child is born.

1/7/1869 Stephen Ulisus Nicks dies.

36

3/2/1869   Mary R. Nicks, their oldest child, marries John J. Hudgins.

11/13/1869 Lilburn McCaslin is born, their 2d grandchild.

11/28/1869 Albert Eugene Hudgins is born, their 3d grandchild.

The American Civil War devastated the South. Most of the war was fought in the South and much of the region's infrastructure was destroyed. Confederate bonds and currency became worthless, depriving the region of a great portion of its wealth. Emancipation of the slaves also destroyed a large part of the South's capital, creating the need for a new labor system. There was little capital available in the South to finance reconstruction, and a slowly growing population did not create a demand for expanded infrastructure, one of the factors driving the rapid expansion of the national economy outside the former Confederate states. For at least 2 generations after the American Civil War, the South remained predominantly agricultural and largely outside the industrial expansion of the national economy. One exception was the development of the iron and steel industry around Birmingham, Alabama.

The iron ore industry already existed in Dickson County and would provide employment for Bart until sometime after 1880. *The Goodspeed History of Dickson County* was published in 1886, 8 years before Bart's death, and states that "Mr. Nicks is a self-made man, and is worth about $8,000." The article continues by stating that he lived about three miles below the furnace and engaged in the raising of livestock.

A net worth of $8,000 at that time in Dickson County would have been a substantial amount. In the 1862 tax assessment list, Bart's 724 acres was valued at $3,600, leaving another $4,400 in assets that could have been livestock, equipment, other land or the value of crops harvested but not sold. Inflation was nonexistent in the country at that time, and, in fact, the country had experienced deflation.

However, a small newspaper article in the *Clarksville Weekly Chronicle* (September 18, 1875, p. 3.) casts a very different light on the financial status of Bart Nicks:

> The residence of Mr. B. W. S. Nicks, situated on the Barton's creek, on the land of Mrs. H. N. Cunningham, was consumed by fire on the 10th of September, together with the greater portion of his household and kitchen furniture. Mr. Nicks is a poor man, and this severe loss calls for assistance from his friends.

This information regarding Bart is in stark contrast to all other information that I have obtained or been told. Reconciling this information to other accounts of his life circumstances is difficult and only highlights the fact that we have very little information regarding his life. *The Goodspeed History of Dickson County* (1886) is generally accepted as an accurate account of the individuals featured in the book. The publication date of an article on B.W.S. is dated 11 years after the fire loss reported in the *Clarksville Weekly Chronicle*, and it is certainly possible that Bart had economically recovered.

The *Clarksville Weekly Chronicle* also states that Bart's residence was on land that he did not own. This is in conflict not only with the 1862 tax assessment, which reports he owned 724 acres, but also with the Schmittou article of 1972. It is possible that the permanent home mentioned in the Schmittou article was built after the reported fire of 1875. The Schmittou home still stands today and is "built around" the original Nicks structure.

It is significant that Bart and America's fourth child, Caleb Newton Nicks, died on October 12, 1875, at the age of 19. This would have been a few days over a month following the date of the reported fire, raising the possibility that the young man died from injuries suffered in the blaze.

The economic conditions that prevailed following the Civil War should also be taken into account when considering the economic status of Bart in 1875. The reconstruction years were very hard on most folks in the South.

Barton Warren Stone passed away on April 8, 1894, and was buried in the Speight/Nicks Cemetery that is located on a hill on the north side of the Stayton Road, across from the home place. America would pass away on March 19, 1905, and is buried beside him. Their grave is marked with a large stone marker that is well over 10 feet tall. Other family members would also be buried there into the 1930s. The cemetery remains today, though in bad repair.

County deed records show that the 7 surviving children of B.W.S. were the heirs of his estate and that the children agreed to sell the home place to two of their siblings, B.W.S. Nicks Jr. and Dora Speight. Dora's husband, Jack, and B.W.S. Jr. were partners in the store known as Speight & Nicks, and the sale was actually titled to the firm. The purchase price is listed as $2,500. Of this price, $1,163 was to be paid to B.W.S. Jr. and Dora Speight to "make them equal to the other heirs under the last will of their father, B. W. S. Nicks, Sr." The balance of the purchase price was $1,337 and was to be paid to all the children, share and share alike, in the following fashion: 1 third to be paid in the first year after the death of their mother, another third due two years after the death of their mother and the final third to be paid 3 years after Mrs. Nicks's death. In addition, Speight & Nicks were to furnish Mrs. Nicks with a comfortable living during her natural lifetime. All of the children except Dora Speight and B.W.S. Jr. signed the deed along with the male spouses of the daughters.

Bart Nicks and America had been among the earliest settlers of Stayton, Tennessee. It was here that they raised their family, and it was here that they were buried. Their children would play a large role in transforming Stayton from a "frontier town" to the center of activity in Northern Dickson County.

Chapter 5
Children of a Settler

The total number of children born to the marriage of B. W. S. Nicks and America Agnes McGraw would be 10, 5 girls and 5 boys. Only 7 would reach adulthood, 1 son died at 23 months of age, another at the age of 19 years and a daughter passed away at 2 years of age.

These children would play important roles in the development of the Stayton area and have a significant impact on the generation that would follow.

Mary R. Nicks was born on November 8, 1848, and was the first child born to B.W.S. and America. It is possible that she was born in either Maury County or Hickman County, but we know through the 1850 census that she then lived with her parents in Montgomery County, Tennessee. She would have been in the household when they moved to Stayton.

On March 2, 1869, at the age of 20, Mary would marry John J. Hudgins. They would have five children, but only two survived to adulthood, a son Albert and a daughter Emma. In May of 1881 they would lose two daughters within four days, Sara, age 8, and Martha, age 6. Sixteen months later, in September of 1882, they would lose another daughter, Iris, when she was 8 years old.

41

Five years later on June 11, 1886, Mary would lose her husband, John. He was 31 years old and left her to raise their two remaining children, Albert, age 17, and Emma, age 14.

Children of Bart and America

Seated L-R: Mary Hudgins, Martha McCaslin, Eudora Speight and Florence Stark. Standing L-R: Henry Clay Nicks, Frank Nicks and Warren Nicks.

Mary was a schoolteacher, first in Stayton and later in Southside, Tennessee, at the Southside Preparatory School. My grandfather, B. C. Nicks, would have been her nephew, and he was educated at the Southside Preparatory School. It was here that he would meet his future bride, Katherine Lyle. The fact that his aunt taught and lived in Southside likely influenced the decision to send B to school there.

On June 22, 1903, Mary Nicks Hudgins passed away, 2 years before her mother died and 26 years after the loss of her husband. She is buried in the Southside Cemetery, and her husband is buried in the old Hudgins Cemetery near Promised Land and the Rodney Owen farm in Dickson County.

Mary's son, Albert Hudgins, would marry Rosa Tidwell. He was well known in Montgomery and Dickson County as a traveling salesman (drummer) of wholesale dry goods and hardware out of Clarksville. He was a first cousin to my grandfather, B. C. Nicks, and was 12 years older. Later, B.C. would have a general merchandise store and Albert called on him. They were close, and Kate Nicks's diary of 1907–8 records that he spent several nights with them while in Dull, a community in northern Dickson County.

Albert and Rosa had a daughter named Emma (8/10/1899–12/16/1982), who was named after Albert's sister. Emma would marry William Orgain of Clarksville, Tennessee. William Orgain was a nephew of Kate Lyle Nicks, and his family founded Orgain Builders Supply Company in Clarksville.

Mary Nicks Hudgins's daughter, also named Emma, was married three times. All of her husbands predeceased her, and she was buried in the Southside Cemetery between two of them. The death and funeral of her second husband is mentioned by Kate Lyle's mother, Elizabeth Lyle, in a letter that was written to Kate in 1909 (Appendix D).

The second child of Bart Nicks and America was born on May 20, 1851, a daughter who was named Martha E. Nicks.

At the age of 15, Martha would marry Benjamin Tidwell McCaslin on December 20, 1866. He had been an officer in the Confederate Army during the war. At the time of their marriage, he was a blacksmith and would later become a merchant who owned and operated the Ben T. McCaslin General Store in Lyles, Tennessee.

To this marriage were born 11 children, and descendants of these children have lived and worked in Dickson and Hickman Counties. Some of our relatives who came from this line would be Lilburn McCaslin, Allen McCaslin, Roy McCaslin, Darby McCaslin Cardona, Lester McCaslin, Dr. Dan McCaslin, Alice Phillips Stone and Stacia Stone Daniel, to name just a few.

On January 23, 1923, at the age of 81, Ben T. McCaslin died in Lyles, Tennessee, from complications of pneumonia. Thirteen years later on February 29, 1936, Martha would pass away from a cerebral hemorrhage. She was 84 years old and still resided in Lyles. Both are buried in Union Cemetery in Dickson, Tennessee.

There are many interrelationships between the McCaslin branch of our family and our branch (Henry Clay Nicks). These relationships were the result of different members of our family marrying into the same family. Some of these family names are Tidwell, Phillips, Speight and Hudgin.

On March 6, 1854, Bart and America's first son was born. They would name him Henry Clay. Henry is my direct ancestor and great grandfather. Henry married Sophronia Rufus Matthews on September 30, 1875. She was the daughter of Buckner Wynn (Buck) Matthews. A later chapter will be devoted to Henry.

Caleb Newton Nicks was the second son and fourth child of B.W.S and America and was born on March 7, 1856. Caleb Newton died on October 13, 1875 at the age of 19 years. We know very little of him. In the 1860 census he is listed as N. Nicks, in the 1870 census as Newton, so we can assume he was called Newton. The 1870 census does not indicate that he attended school during the preceding 12 months. This census does indicate that Newton could read and write but also indicates that his younger brother by two years could not. Ruth Nicks Hunt, in her genealogical book on our family, states that he was buried at the old Henry Hooper Farm Cemetery near Charlotte. As of this date (2017) I have been unable to locate this cemetery, but I believe the Nicks family utilized it prior to B.W.S.'s passing when the Nicks/Speight Cemetery in Stayton was then established.

It should be noted that the date of Newton's death is 33 days after a fire destroyed his father's home, as reported in the *Clarksville Weekly Chronicle.* His death was also 13 days after the marriage of Henry Clay Nicks and Sophronia Matthews.

The fifth child born into this family was also a son, James Franklin Nicks, who was born on January 22, 1858. He was known by the family as Uncle Frank, and he owned and worked a large farm in Stayton. Most of the farm is presently owned by his descendants, Steven and Julie Sensing. *Goodspeed History of Dickson County* states that Frank farmed all his life, beginning at age 19, that his education was limited, but that he made the most of his opportunities and that he was a member of the Christian Church.[44]

Frank married Eliza Harriet Bartee on December 24, 1879. Eliza was born on December 13, 1860. She was an ancestor of John Bartee of Clarksville, who was one of the most able and best-known County Extension Agents in the U.T. Extension Service. John was admired statewide for his work with young people and the local farmers of Montgomery County.

Most of the descendants of Frank Nicks who are presently known in Dickson County came from his second child, a daughter, named Addie Lee. She was born 6/6/1883 and married William Dillard on 12/29/1908. This marriage produced a daughter, Mary Elizabeth Dillard, born 4/29/1910, and she married John D. Sensing Sr. John D. Sensing succeeded James Nicks, a grandson of Henry Clay Nicks, as Chairman of the Dickson County Board of Education. John D. and Mary Elizabeth had a son named John D. Sensing Jr., who was a teacher and coach in the Dickson County School System for many years. John Jr.'s children, Steven and Julie, presently own the property farmed by Frank Nicks over 138 years ago.

Frank's third child, Eula Agnes Nicks, would marry Dr. William H. Cunningham, who was the local physician in Stayton and was the primary doctor for many in our family. He would also have been the physician who signed many of the death certificates in the area.

To Frank and Eliza would be born 11 children; four would die as children or infants, two would live to marry but would have no children and only Addie Lee would raise her family in Dickson County.

On September 28, 1927, at the age of 69, Uncle Frank would pass away due to pneumonia that was brought on by complications of paralysis. It is not known if the paralysis was due to an accident or resulted from a stroke. His son-in-law, Dr. Cunningham, signed the death certificate.

Twenty-one years later at the age of 88, Eliza would die of carcinoma of the stomach. She was still residing in the Stayton area at the time of her death. Both Frank and Eliza are buried in the Nicks/Speight Cemetery in Stayton.

Eudora Ann Nicks was the sixth child born to Bart and America during the first 12 years of their marriage. She was born on November 22, 1859 and was the third daughter born to the family. In 1882, at the age of 22 years, she would marry John M. (Jack) Speight, who was born on January 7, 1856.

Jack was born in White Bluff, Tennessee, and at the age of 17 (1874) went to live with his uncle, Ben T. McCaslin.[45] McCaslin had married Bart Nicks's second child, Martha E. Nicks. Ben McCaslin's sister was Jack Speight's mother. Jack went to live with his Uncle Ben to learn the trade of blacksmithing.[46] When Jack married Eudora, who was Martha's younger sister, he became the brother-in-law of his uncle, Ben T. McCaslin.

Jack would remain with his Uncle until 1876, when he left to work for the railroad. After about a year he returned to his Uncle and resumed his work as a blacksmith. Eighteen months later he would leave again, this time for Fulton, Kentucky, where he continued to practice blacksmithing. After about two years, he returned to Stayton and bought Ben T. McCaslin's blacksmith shop. He remained with this business until 1884, when he entered the merchandising business with his brother-in-law, B.W.S. Nicks Jr. (known as Warren).[47, 48]

As a child, my Dad and I would sometimes ride to Stayton, not to visit anyone in particular (no family was left to visit), but just to see Grandpa's house. Every time we would go, Dad would point out this large Victorian house in Stayton and say, "That was Jack Speight's house, he did very well." John Speight was called Jack by all who knew him. He was a farmer, blacksmith, landowner, landlord, merchant, undertaker, banker and investor.

Much of what he accomplished was in partnership with his brother-in-law, Barton Warren Stone Nicks Jr., who was 7½ years younger than Jack.

The story of Jack and Dora's marriage and his relationship with his brother-in-law Warren Nicks is very interesting and will be covered in later chapters.

On December 24, 1861, America would give birth to their seventh child, a daughter named Elenora W. Nicks. She would pass away on May 4, 1864, prior to her third birthday. This was the first of two children they would lose as infants. This information is from the family Bible that is in the possession of Sammy Nicks.

The eighth of their ten children was born on June 25, 1863, a boy named Barton Warren Stone Nicks Jr., the same that would be known as Warren.

Warren would marry Dottie Elinavent Phillips, who was born on September 11, 1873. Dottie was the daughter of Cave Phillips and Jane Matthews Phillips. Jane Matthews and my great grandmother Sophronia Matthews were sisters. In other words, Warren married his sister-in-law's niece. Dottie had a brother,

47

Rufus Slayden Phillips, who would marry Martha Nicks McCaslin's daughter, Florence McCaslin.

Two children were born to Warren and Dottie. The oldest was a daughter named Helon Nicks (8/27/1899–7/11/1941), who married George Brown Harris. This couple had no children. George Harris was a son of Thomas Wetherstone Harris and Sarah Heard.

The Harrises had two other children who would marry into the Nicks family: a son named Daniel Heard Harris, who would marry Henry Clay Nicks's daughter Evie, becoming the parents of Margaret Little and Agnes Boyce. The Harrises also had a daughter, Mary, who would marry Hubert Stark, whose mother, Florence Nicks was a daughter of B.W.S. Sr. On a side note, the Harrises had another son, Bob, who was the father of Mary Ann Self, Coach Milton Self's wife.

Warren's son was named Robert Herschel Nicks (10/6/1906–7/19/1981) who married Edith Milam. They had two sons, Glen Nicks and James (Jimmy) Nicks. Herschel had a nickname, Penal, and he had quite a checkered past, especially in his youth. He served some time in prison for selling large amounts of rationed sugar during WWII.

Warren Nicks would pass away on December 23, 1935, from a stroke that was complicated by pneumonia. He was buried the following day in the Nicks/Speight Cemetery, with arrangements by Taylor Funeral Home. Warren was a very successful businessman and merchant and had accumulated land and other investments during his life.

Florence America Nicks would be the last child born to B.W.S. and America that would live to adulthood. She was born on September 25, 1865. On October 30, 1881, she married Elijah Washington Stark (6/16/1858–6/10/1935). He was a farmer as well as a partner in the mercantile business with Slayden Phillips. Their farm would have been on the north side of Barton's creek, located on what today is known as Stark Road. It is a beautiful, fertile farm blessed with Barton Creek bottomland.

Elijah and Florence would have three sons: Thomas Wilmore Stark, Barton Hubert Stark and Clifford Nicks Stark. Hubert Stark would marry Mary Harris and they had three sons: Tom, Dan and Joe. All were very well thought of, and our family stayed in touch with them through the years. I was well acquainted with Tom; he was well-informed regarding our family history and was kind enough to share the picture of B.W.S. Nicks and America that belonged to his family. This is the only picture of B.W.S. that I know to exist.

The third son of Elijah and Florence Stark was Clifford Stark, who was a college professor at Ithaca College in Ithaca, N.Y., and later at M.T.S.U. in Murfreesboro. Dr. Stark and his wife left their family farm to M.T.S.U., and the Agribusiness building at M.T.S.U. was named in his honor. Mrs. Dena Sullivan of Dickson was his secretary in the 1950s while she attended M.T.S.U.

On October 10, 1867, the last of Bart and America's children was born. Stephen Ulisus Nicks was the youngest child of Bart and America, and he would die on January 7, 1869, at 15 months of age. He is buried in a cemetery located at the "old Henry Hooper farm" near Charlotte, where many of those who passed away before B.W.S. were buried there. The descendants of Barton Warren Stone Nicks and America Agnes McGraw would have a profound impact on the Stayton community and the people who lived there. They were responsible for much of the economic, social and spiritual development of this area that was known as the hub of the North Side of Dickson County. Their impact on the future of indigent children was as great as their impact on commerce.

Children of Bart Nicks, with Spouses, circa 1900

1st Row L to R: Henry Clay Nicks, Sophronia Nicks, Dora Speight & Jack Speight. 2nd Row, Martha McCaslin, Warren Nicks, America Agnes Nicks, Florence Stark, Thomas Stark. 3rd Row – Ben T. McCaslin, Mary Hudgins, Frank Nicks, Eliza Nicks

Chapter 6
Bound Children

For the greater part of the 1800's, orphans and children of families unable to provide for their care were apprenticed or bound out to a trade. Sometimes a family voluntarily gave up a child, but in many instances, the matter would be brought to the County court. In other cases, a family in need would reach out to relatives to seek the care needed to raise a child. Many times the need for assistance resulted from single parent families.

Most of these children were without resources and often without advocates. Local officials undertook the responsibility for putting such children in family situations where the child was expected to work, while the master provided an education and the basic living needs. The adoption practices with which we are familiar today did not exist in the 1800s, but the need for childcare did.

There are three known instances where our family assumed the responsibility of raising children in need. These cases involved two of our ancestral families and they all occurred prior to 1900.

Bart and America Nicks assumed responsibility for two children through a Dickson County Court proceeding in 1884. Minutes of these court proceedings show that Sid Deloach appeared in Court to request that the Court "take charge of his children." William Thomas Deloach, six years of age and his sister Mary Ann Deloach, four years old were placed into the care of Bart and America. Sid Deloach specifically requested that the Court "bind them to one B. W. S. Nicks."[49]

The U. S. Census records of 1890 were destroyed by a fire, leaving us with little information on the changes in households between 1880 and 1900. Since Bart died in 1894, the last record we have of him as head of the household is the 1880 census. Sixteen years would lapse between the adoption of the Deloach children in 1884 and the next census that was conducted in 1900.

William Thomas and Josie Deloach

By 1900, Barton Nicks had died and America was living in the household with her daughter and her son-in-law, Dora and Jack Speight. Included in this household was William Thomas Deloach.

He was then 22 years of age, single and his relationship to the family is listed as "servant." His occupation is noted as a farm laborer. On December 31, 1900, William Thomas would marry Josie Hayes. William and Josie would live their lives in the Stayton, Tennessee, area and would have a large family of eleven children.

Their second child would be a son born in 1906, named Clarence Thomas Deloach, who would be the father of Clarence Thomas Deloach Jr., who would become a Church of Christ minister that preached at Walnut Street Church of Christ during the 1990s.

William Thomas Deloach passed away on December 3, 1955, at the age of 78 from a stroke that occurred in Nashville. He was still a resident of Stayton and was buried in the Deloach Cemetery. His death certificate was signed by Dr. W. A. Crosby.

Josie would continue to live in the Stayton area and would pass away on October 15, 1973. No further details regarding her death have been found to date, but it is almost a certainty that she would have been buried next to her husband.

Jack and Eudora (Nicks) Speight

The Census of 1900 provides another piece of valuable information with respect to "adopted" children. Even though Jack and Dora Speight had no children of their own, their extended family presents an interesting story. Jack Speight and Dora Nicks were married in 1882. Because of the destruction of the Federal Census records of 1890, the first record that we have of them as a married couple is found in the 1900 census.

The 1900 census lists John M. Speight (this is Jack) as the head of the household, 44 years old, and his occupation is listed as a merchant. Eudora is listed as his wife, age 40, no occupation listed. Also included in the household listing are:

Arthur Speight, age 9, was born in August of 1890. He is listed as a nephew and shown as attending school.

Rosie Powell, a young girl of 8 years was born in September of 1891. She is listed as "bound" and as attending school.

America Nicks, age 68, born in October 1831. This is Dora's mother and the widow of Bart Nicks.

Leah A. Nesbitt, age 64, was born in May 1836. She is listed as a boarder and as widowed. This is a sister of America Agnes Nicks.

William T. Deloach, age 22, who was born in March 1878, is listed as a servant and farm laborer. Thomas was discussed previously in this chapter.

Arthur Speight was Jack's nephew and was raised by Jack and Dora. He was the son of Jack Speight's younger brother, Albert Franklin Speight. The exact reason for his "adoption" into Jack's household is unknown; however, census data, court records and city directories provide information that allows us to draw some conclusions regarding these circumstances.

Albert Franklin Speight was one year younger than his brother, Jack. He was known as A.F. In 1889, A.F. would marry Amelia Jones, and in August of 1890 Arthur would be born. Sometime in 1892 Amelia passed away and A. F. would be left a widower with a son that was less than two years old. It would be most likely that sometime after his mother's death Arthur would enter the household of his Uncle Jack.

Arthur's father, A.F., would later marry Caroline (Carrie) Simpson and they would live in Clarksville, Tennessee where they would raise three other sons. There is no evidence that Arthur ever moved back into his father's household.

On May 21, 1939, A. F. would pass away in Clarksville, Tennessee. He is buried in the Greenwood Cemetery that is located in Clarksville. In his will he left his estate to a son named Clarence, who was his business partner. Census data lists A.F.'s occupation as a contractor.

The will also specifically mentions three other sons, Albert, Arthur and Carl. To these sons he left one dollar each but also canceled any indebtedness that they may have owed him.

It would appear that while Arthur remained in the household of his Uncle Jack, he would have continued to have some contact with his biological father. The forgiveness of indebtedness in a will indicates that the indebtedness was never paid. None of these facts would lead one to believe that the relationship between Arthur and his father was a close one.

After 1900, Arthur would appear in Jack and Dora's household in both the 1910 and 1920 censuses. In 1910 Arthur is again listed as a nephew; however, in the 1920 census he is listed as adopted.

Arthur was a veteran of World War I, and before his time in the service he worked for his Uncle Jack and Warren Nicks in their undertaking business. His early education occurred at the Stayton School. Later, he would train as a mechanic. Prior to 1930 he would marry Katherine Taylor, daughter of Thomas Taylor, one of the brothers that founded Taylor Brothers Funeral Home. In the 1930 census Arthur and his wife were living at 318 Main Street in Dickson and designated a mechanic.

In 1942 Arthur was killed in an automobile accident. His wife, Kate, thereafter worked as a sales clerk in a dry goods store in Dickson until her death in 1951. They are both buried in Dickson's Union Cemetery in the Taylor family plot.

The census of 1900 also lists another child living in the household of Jack and Dora who was named Rosa Powell. She was eight years old at the time, having been born in September of 1891. Rosa is listed as "bound." I have found no records that would indicate who her parents were or any particulars regarding her "adoption."

The 1910 census of Jack Speight's family does not list Rosa. She would have been 17 years old at that time, and it is possible that she was away at school or living somewhere else.

In the 1920 census Rosa reappears in the Jack Speight household. She is now 27 years of age and her relationship to the family has changed from "bound" to "adopted child." This change does not necessarily mean that there was a change in her legal status, but more likely reflected a change in census terminology.

Jack Speight is listed as the head of the household in 1920 and was then 64 years old. His occupation is listed as the operator of his farm. There was no occupation listed for his wife, Dora, or for Rosa. In the next chapter, I will discuss merchandising during this era, but I believe Jack's change in occupation from merchant to farmer is significant considering the economic changes that were occurring in 1920.

On March 19, 1925, at the age of 65 years, Eudora Nicks Speight passed away. Dr. Cunningham of the Stayton community signed her death certificate that stated she "died before medical attention could reach her—she had high blood pressure." Her occupation was listed as homemaker on the death certificate. Jack, who was 69 years old, provided the information contained in the death certificate and Taylor Brothers was in charge of the funeral arrangements. Dora is buried in the Nicks/Speight Cemetery alongside of her mother and father, Bart and America Nicks.

Later that same year, in Davidson County, Jack Speight and Rosa Powell were married. I have found a copy of the marriage certificate on a Davidson County search site, but the image is too small to be reproduced.

No one in my family ever spoke to me of this marriage and, at least in our family, their story is unusual. Jack had no children by either marriage. Without descendants, Rosa's whole life might well have been forgotten. I spent a little over a year researching records in an effort to discover the rest of her story.

Jack was 69 years old when Dora passed away; Rosa was 32. The death certificate indicates that Dora's death was sudden. Her departure would present several problems with respect to how Jack and Rosa would conduct their lives moving forward.

Rosa had spent most of her life in Jack's household. Her absence in the 1910 census when she was 17 years of age does not necessarily mean that she had left the household. It was common for census takers to omit individuals who were absent on the day of the visit. She may have been at school. In any case, in the 1920 census, she was again listed in the household, and her return may have been to provide care for two aging people who were the only parents she had ever known.

It does not take a lot of imagination to envision the possible response of friends and family to the situation of a 69-year-old stepfather cohabiting with his 32-year-old stepdaughter. Given Jack's position in the community, I believe they would have been sensitive to the situation. Where was Rosa to go? After years of living in this household, was she to leave simply because her stepmother had died? In addition, who would have provided the daily care needed for Jack? After years of caring for orphans and widows, Jack himself was suddenly alone and in need of care. It should not be forgotten that, in those years, long-term care outside the home was not available.

Additionally, Jack Speight had been a very successful businessman and had accumulated a sizable net worth. What would happen to his assets at his death? He had no children, except for his adopted family. Regardless of his net worth, his overriding need was for someone to care for him during his last years.

It is my opinion that Jack and Rosa decided to care for each other as family, and the only honorable way they could do that would have been to marry. Rosa would take care of Jack for the rest of his life, and he would leave the majority of his estate to her at his death. This solution would have been consistent with the moral and religious beliefs that Jack would have held as an active member of his church and community. It would also settle the issue of asset distribution at his death. On March 19, 1930, John M. (Jack) Speight died of carcinoma of the stomach. The attending physician was Dr. Cunningham of Stayton. The death certificate states that Jack was under Dr. Cunningham's care from January 1, 1928, until the day of his death. He had apparently dealt with this disease for over two years. He was buried the following day in the Nicks/Speight Cemetery next to his first wife, Dora. Taylor Brothers Funeral Home was in charge of the arrangements.

On May 12, 1930, the last will and testament of John M. Speight was entered into the probate court of Judge Joe B. Weems. In accordance with his will, Mrs. Rosa Powell Speight was named executrix, and Clyde Smith was named as co-executor. Clyde Smith was the cashier of the Stayton Bank & Trust Company. The will was dated on September 16, 1927. A codicil was attached and made a part of the will. Both documents were witnessed by B. W. S. (Warren) Nicks Jr. and Warren's son-in-law, George B. Harris.

Jack's will left the majority of his assets to Rosa. Jack had a sister named Sallie Dendy to whom he left $500. To his nephew, Arthur Speight, he left a house and lot on Cullum Street in Dickson and the sum of $1,000, to be paid in semi-annual payments of $100.

The remainder was to be given to Rosa. This included a 200-acre farm that was the Bart Nicks home place and a 111-acre farm that he had purchased at a tax sale. He also left Rosa a house with two lots located in the Lokeland development of East Nashville. This house is located at the corner of Woodland and 17th Streets and would become Rosa's home once the estate was settled.

He further bequeathed to Rosa his interest in the Stayton Telephone Company and a factory building and lot located in Cumberland Furnace, Tennessee.

Rosa was also to receive all of his personal property. An inventory of these items was filed with the court when the estate was closed. These items included 4½ shares of the International Life Insurance Company, 8 shares of the Stayton Bank & Trust Company, 10 shares of the Tennessee Electric Power Company, a $1,300 U.S. Liberty Bond yielding 4½ percent and a time deposit in the Stayton Bank of $8,500. Also included were the notes of A. F. Speight & Son for $2,000 and a $1,000 note of R. V. Schmittou securing the purchase of the Bart Nicks home and farm.

The holdings of telephone, utility and life insurance companies give insight into how life had changed in rural Tennessee during the first 30 years of the 20th Century.

During the period that the estate was open, a document was filed with the court that stated the Schmittou note had been paid in full. This document sheds light on the disposition of the B. W. S. Nicks home place. The importance of this property in terms of our family history lies in the fact that we believe that B. W. S. Nicks Sr. was one of the first residents to settle in Stayton, and we know where this farm is located.

In his article regarding the early settlers of Stayton, Earl V. Schmittou states that his home place is the old farm of Bart Nicks, whose family settled in Stayton during the 1850s. Mr. Schmittou also states that his family purchased this property from Jack Speight in the fall of 1927. The court records that I have been able to find seem to validate this, and they show that the transaction came about in the following fashion.

After the death of B. W. S. Nicks in 1894, the home place was equally divided among Bart's children. Later, Jack Speight and Warren Nicks purchased all of the children's shares and the property was transferred to Speight & Nicks. On August 30, 1927, B. W. S. Nicks Jr. (Warren) transferred his half undivided interest in the tract to Jack Speight.

On November 23, 1927, Jack Speight entered into an agreement to sell the home place to Rufus V. Schmittou for a price of $6,500 and to take a note from Mr. Schmittou for payment that was secured by a mortgage on the property. On January 1, 1928, the Schmittou family took possession of the property. All of these transfers began about the time that Jack first became ill.

Jack's will leaves the described property to his wife, Rosa. There was still indebtedness against the property, and Jack would have viewed such as an asset that required disposition. When the Schmittou family paid the remaining balance on the note, Rosa executed a proper deed transferring the property to them.

Later, this property would transfer from Mrs. Rufus Schmittou to her son, Earl V. Schmittou Sr., who would then later transfer ownership to his son, Earl V. Schmittou Jr.

To comprehend the scope and size of Jack's holdings, one must understand the value of things in 1930. According to the IRS, 50 percent of those filing income tax returns in 1930 made less than $3,000 per year. According to the Web site *The People History*, bread cost 8 cents a loaf, potatoes were 18 cents for 10 pounds and Campbell's Tomato Soup was four cans for 25 cents. Gasoline was less than 20 cents a gallon and the average home cost less than $4,000. Jack's assets at his death were sizable.

These were the last records that I had been able to find regarding Jack and Roas Speight in the Dickson County Courthouse. For some time I searched for property records and real estate transfers in her name; I found nothing. There were no death records or cemetery records that would lead me to determine what had happened to Rosa Powell Speight or her assets.

The 1930 census was taken on April 4, 1930, 15 days after Jack had passed away. This census lists Rosa Speight as the head of the household, and living with her sister-in-law Sallie Dendy, sister of Jack Speight, also a widow. (Interesting note: 10 years later in the same house, the 1940 census has Percy Speight living in this house. Percy was a nephew of Jack, and Dendy was still residing there. Percy would later marry Decima Speight, who would teach English at Dickson High School.)

Beyond this, I was finding no trace of Rosa. She did not appear in any of the 1940 census data for Dickson or Davidson County (where she had inherited a home in East Nashville). I had been searching for about 6 months and told a friend of mine who does genealogical research about my frustrations. Two weeks later, she provided me with a newspaper article from the June 30, 1933, issue of the *Dickson County Herald*:

Announcement is made of the marriage of Mrs. Rosa P. Speight, of Stayton, and John T. Carpenter, of Nashville, which was solemnized June 20th, in the study of the officiating minister, Rev. D. M. Walker, Hopkinsville, Ky. The bride's niece, Miss Mabel Speight, of Cumberland Furnace, and Frank Mitchell, of Clarksville were the attendants. After the ceremony, Mr. and Mrs. Carpenter left for an eastern bridal trip and are now at home at 1711 Russell St., Nashville.

Mr. Carpenter was 59 years of age when they married, 19 years older than Rosa, who was 40 years old at the time. The house where they made their home on Russell Street is in the same neighborhood in East Nashville as the house Rosa received in her inheritance under the will of Jack Speight.

In 1920 the census in Davidson County says that Mr. Carpenter was then 46 years old and lived at the same address on Russell Street and worked as a mail clerk for the railroad. He was married and his wife was 40 at that time.

In the 1940 census John T. Carpenter was 66 old and Rosa was 47. They resided at his home on Russell Street, and neither of them indicated that they were employed. By 1945 Nashville city directories indicate they lived at 929 Caldwell Lane, and a Nashville city directory of 1951 has them at the same address. This is in the area of David Lipscomb University, close to Granny White Pike.

On May 13, 1953, Rosa Powell Speight Carpenter would pass away. Her death certificate states the cause of death as carcinoma of the stomach. She had been under the care of a physician for 10 to 12 weeks. Jack Speight had died from this same disease.

The death certificate indicates she was a widow. We know through Nashville City Directories that Mr. Carpenter was alive in 1951, meaning she would have been a widow for two years or less. She had undergone surgery for her condition in March of 1953. At the time of her death she was still a resident at 929 Caldwell Lane and was 60 years old. The death certificate states that the names of her mother and father were unknown. The informant listed on the certificate was a Louise Speight. (This is the wife of one of Jack's nephews.)

Rosa is buried at Woodlawn Cemetery in the plot of a Monroe family. Mr. Monroe was a dentist in Nashville, and one of his sons was a friend of Rosa's who donated the plot. This information is from the files at Woodlawn Cemetery. A grave marker was provided by the wife of Jack's nephew, Louise Speight. Rosa's grave location is Chapel Garden B, Lot 228, Space 4.

The funeral arrangements were handled by Phillips, Robinson Funeral Home. Rosa's first husband, John M. (Jack) Speight, had a nephew who also went by the name of Jack Speight. This is very confusing, and going forward I will refer to the nephew as Jack the Nephew.

According to records at the funeral home, Jack the Nephew took responsibility for payment of Rosa's funeral, which was $693.13. The funeral home records also show that $35.00 was paid on the bill and the remainder was charged off as uncollectable. The nephew Jack Speight had a reputation of being somewhat irresponsible.

Rosa left a will that was probated in Davidson County on June 23, 1953, naming Clyde Smith of Stayton as her executor. This same Clyde Smith had for years been in the employ of Stayton Bank & Trust Company and had served as co-executor with Rosa in the settlement of Jack Speight's estate.

Her first instruction in the will states that Mr. Smith, as her executor, should pay for her funeral expenses. Her second request was that Mr. Smith select, purchase and erect a monument for her grave. Mr. Smith fulfilled neither of these requests.

Rosa then set instruction for the division of her property. It was her wish that the assets of her second husband be divided among his living children. The assets that she had inherited from her first husband, Jack Speight, was to be divided among Jack the nephew and Martha Phillips Frake, who were both relatives of Rosa's first husband. This division of property left those assets she had received from Jack Speight to his relatives and assets she received from Mr. Carpenter to his daughters.

The final clause in her will reads as follows; "In preparation of this will I have not been unmindful of the interests and claims of my blood kin, but have intentionally omitted them for the reason that this property came to me from former husbands, and I am respecting their requests in the preparation of this will."

This final statement in Rosa's will is interesting because it alludes to the fact that she had "blood kin" that were known to her. While her death certificate states her mother and father were unknown, that does not mean Rosa was unaware of the identity of her parents. It only means that the informant on the certificate did not know. I have found no information that indicates her "blood kin" took any part in her final arrangements. To date I have not located anyone who would have been a blood relative.

As interesting as Rosa's story is, the only person involved who is of our family was Eudora Nicks Speight. The fact that Rosa was listed as "bound" in the 1900 census was what first fascinated me. I think her story is compelling. I hope that Dora would want it told. I also believe that Rosa loved her stepfather and stepmother and was happy in her later years with Mr. Carpenter. I have found no record of Mr. Carpenter's death.

Chapter 7
Economic Growth and Merchandising

In rural Middle Tennessee, prior to 1880, almost every head of a household was listed in census data as a farmer or farm laborer. The availability of stock goods was scarce, and most families grew what they ate and made the items necessary for their clothing. Consumer items that were available for sale were rare. Those items that were available were transported into the community by teamsters or wagoners on return trips from hauling goods produced locally to larger markets. Our family was involved in this transportation of goods during the 1840s and into 1850s. This early trade of goods would become the earliest beginnings of what would later become known as "general merchandising."

The United States fell into economic depression with the Panic of 1873 and would not begin to recover fully until 1885. During this period of economic stress, farm prices would fall to historic lows, yet the production of steel would increase significantly. The Industrial Revolution had begun.

Middle Tennessee saw progressive changes in the years between the end of Reconstruction in 1877 and 1900. The landscape was transformed by the beginnings of large-scale industry, the emergence of small-town life, the spread of general stores and the sudden rise of the railroads.[50]

In 1891, the L&N Railroad built the Mineral Branch from Pond Switch to Clarksville. This line came off the Nashville-to-Memphis route just west of Dickson and included a 6-mile spur to Cumberland Furnace. The accessibility of rail service would change those communities affected, such as Sylvia, Vanleer, Stayton, Lone Oak and Clarksville. The availability of goods and services heretofore unknown to these rural residents increased dramatically and life in the rural communities would never be the same.

New products and services would increase the need for retail outlets, and the general store would become a mainstay of community life. By the turn of the century, the South contained about 144 stores per county.[51]

While there was an increase in consumption and consumerism, money was in short supply because most of the residents farmed for a living with most of their produce used for personal consumption. Since there were few if any banks at the time, credit fell to the local merchant, who in turn would need credit from his supplier, the wholesale grocer.

Credit would be supplied to the farmer on an annual basis for the supplies needed to raise a crop and for the spending money that would be needed during the year. This credit would be secured by the crop being raised and often by a mortgage on the farmer's land. Interest rates charged were high, and if the farmer could not pay his annual bill, he risked foreclosure.

If a foreclosure occurred, the merchant would become the owner of the land, often retaining the farmer as a tenet. This, then, placed the merchant in the position of both seller of goods and landlord of property. These arrangements would result in Jack Speight and Warren Nicks being the owners of several farms in the area.

Stayton began to grow and prosper and became known for its schools, a baseball team, a brass band that traveled throughout the area and its churches. Several doctors practiced there during the late 1800s, and Stayton had the first chartered bank in the county in about 1903. Stayton was considered the hub of the north side of Dickson County, and according to Earl Schmittou, "At one time the descendants of B. W. S. Nicks Sr. comprised the majority of the population of Stayton"[52]

Our Nicks family would play a large role in the development and growth of general merchandising and the wholesale grocery business in Dickson County and the surrounding area.

Those of our family, by birth and marriage, who were involved in the merchandising business during this period were Cave Johnson Phillips, Ben T. McCaslin, Elijah Washington Stark, John M. (Jack) Speight, B. W. S. (Warren) Nicks, Jr., Slayden Phillips and Anthony Matthews. They are all interrelated, as most of these individuals either were descendants of Bart Nicks or had married into his family.Cave Phillips was the oldest of these men, being born in 1842. He was the first to open a general store in the Stayton community, known as C. J. Phillips & Son. The exact date of the opening of this store is unknown but is believed to be around 1880. This store was first located on Fatty Bread branch, in front of the Phillips home. Later, the store was moved into the town of Stayton and would become known as the Stark-Phillips store when Elijah Washington Stark became a partner. It should be noted that Elijah Washington Stark was married to Bart's youngest daughter, Florence. Later, in about 1910, the store would be known as Phillips Brothers, and it was owned and operated by Cave Phillips's son, Slayden Phillips and his family.

Ben McCaslin would first work as a blacksmith and specialized in the making of wagon wheels. Sometime around 1882 he would sell this business to his nephew, John M. (Jack) Speight.

Ben then moved to Lyles, Tennessee, in Hickman County and opened the Ben T. McCaslin General Merchandise store there.

The second general-merchandise business to open in Stayton was the Speight/Nicks General Merchandise Store. This establishment was opened in about 1884 by John M. (Jack) Speight and Barton Warren Stone Nicks Jr. These men were brothers-in-law, Jack having married Warren's older sister, Eudora Nicks.

This business was known as Speight/Nicks and was a large general merchandising store. This large store offered a wide array of products and traded in everything from locally grown produce to cast-iron stoves manufactured in the North to harness tanned in St. Louis. Some of the services offered were blacksmithing, a barbershop, a wide array of dry goods including men's suits and a millinery department. In 1900 Stayton's first Post Office was located in this store.

The sizable business also served the farm community with hardware, fertilizer, seed, farm machinery, wagons and buggies and a complete line of groceries. At one time this establishment employed 11 clerks.[53]

The store also carried a line of caskets that were bought in the rough and had to be trimmed out and finished before being used for burial purposes. In those days, the viewing would be done in the home, with services held at a local church. Speight and Nicks began an undertaking company and first used a horse-drawn hearse, which was later replaced by a motor hearse.

General stores that carried an inventory of caskets would align themselves with larger funeral homes in the area. Speight/Nicks had such an arrangement with Taylor Brothers Funeral Home in Dickson. Later, as burial regulations became more stringent, these stores would act as referral units for the funeral homes, and this arrangement developed between Speight/Nicks and Taylor Brothers Funeral Home. Some of the early death certificates in this area indicate that Speight/Nicks

Company was responsible for the burial and that Taylor Brothers served as the funeral director.

The Stark-Phillips General Merchandise store and the Speight-Nicks General Merchandise Store were in direct competition and were located practically next door to each other. The owners of these two stores were also connected through the Nicks Family in various ways. These relationships provide insight into the impact that Bart Nicks's children and their spouses had on the early economic development of the Stayton Community.

Cave Phillips was married to Jane Matthews. She was the middle child of Bucker W. (Buck) Matthews. Buck had a son, Anthony A. Matthews, who was older than Jane, and a daughter, Sophronia Rufus, who was the youngest.

Cave and Jane would have 11 children, but we will only concern ourselves with the two oldest, Rufus Slayden Phillips and Dottie Elinavent Phillips. Slayden Phillips would marry Florence Eudora McCaslin, the daughter of Ben T. McCaslin and Martha E. Nicks, daughter of Bart Nicks. Dottie Elinavent Phillips would marry Barton Warren Stone Nicks Jr., a son of Bart Nicks.

Buck Matthews's youngest daughter, Sophronia Rufus, would marry Henry Clay Nicks, a direct ancestor in my line. Henry is a son of Bart Nicks.

Additionally, Jack Speight, the partner of Warren Nicks in the Speight-Nicks store, was married to Eudora Nicks, a daughter of Bart Nicks. There is more.

At some point in time, Cave Phillips sold a portion of his store to Elijah Washington Stark, and the store became known as Stark-Phillips & Co. This store remained adjacent to the Speight-Nicks store, and they remained competitors. Elijah Washington Stark married Florence Nicks, a daughter of Bart Nicks.

As mentioned earlier, Buckner W. (Buck) Matthew had three children, two girls and a boy. As stated, his younger daughter, Sophronia, married Henry Clay Nicks, which makes her my great grandmother. Buck's son, Anthony Matthews, was active and successful in the wholesale grocery business in Nashville, Tennessee. He would also have an influence on later generations in terms of merchandising.

Anthony Amariah Matthews

Anthony Matthews was born on Barton's Creek in Dickson County, and during his early years worked at various jobs. He sold fruit trees, farmed, managed the Cumberland Furnace Farm, was a Constable, served as Postmaster in Bellsburg and was a clerk in the Cumberland Furnace Store. For a short while he would be in the general store with his brother-in-law, Cave Johnson Phillips in Stayton. When he left Stayton, he then went

70

into business in Nashville, where he found his calling in the wholesale grocery business. Anthony would be in partners with several associates during his career, one of which would be his nephew, A. J. Phillips. A.J. was a son of Cave and Jane Phillips. The company would then be known as Matthews, Phillips & Co.

Prior to the influx of the railroads, the transport of goods into Nashville was either by wagon or riverboat. Riverboats would come into Nashville on the Cumberland River, where docks were located on the River in the general area of Broadway and First Avenue.

In order to be convenient to these docks, many wholesale houses were located in this area. Anthony Matthews located his earliest warehouse on Second Avenue (Market Street) in close proximity to these loading areas.

As railroads become more prominent, more and more goods were arriving and departing from the Union Station area. This would require merchants to hire wagons to deliver their goods to and from the rail station to their warehouses.

Located adjacent to Union Station, Cummins Station was built as an industrial warehouse that would allow wholesalers to take advantage of the rail systems. This structure was built by William J. Cummins, the chairman of the Bon Air Coal & Iron Corporation. Upon completion in 1906 it was the largest concrete industrial warehouse in the world. The enormous structure was divided into sections that were then sold much like condominium units are today. Anthony Matthews purchased the fourth unit, and the address of Matthews & Phillips was then known as Cummins #4, Nashville, Tennessee. Cummins Station has been on the National Register of Historic Places since November 17, 1983.

Anthony was prominent in the Nashville community. He served one term as the State Senator representing Davidson County and was highly regarded both professionally and personally in the Nashville Community.[54]

71

Anthony A. Matthews would pass away on April 26, 1912, at the age of 63. According to his death certificate, his cause of death was chronic tuberculosis. Funeral services were held at the Christ Episcopal Church (now cathedral) in Nashville, and his burial was at Mt. Olive Cemetery in Nashville. His pall bearers included the Honorable E. E. Howse, Mayor of Nashville, the Honorable M. R. Patterson, former Governor of Tennessee, C. T. Cheek, a prominent merchant who developed Maxwell House Coffee and whose family later built Cheekwood Mansion, Robert Orr, founder of the wholesale grocery firm of Robert Orr & Sons, R. B. Stone, a former manager of Cumberland Furnace, J. W. Napier, a prominent Nashville businessman whose family had built the Tennessee Furnace near Stayton, and Thomas W. Harris, a neighbor and former merchant in Stayton.[55]

Knowledge of and connections to a large wholesale grocery concern would be critical to the success of the general merchandising stores in the smaller communities. There can be little doubt that the generations of our family who pursued merchandising as a trade would have depended on Anthony Matthews, both for advice and access to credit.

Beyond merchandising, Jack Speight and Warren Nicks would have other impacts on the economic growth of Stayton. In about 1902 they would determine that a Bank was necessary to the continued growth of the area. Along with other local shareholders, B. W. S. Nicks Jr. and Jack Speight formed the Stayton Bank & Trust Company. B. W. S. Nicks Jr. would serve as the president of the bank from its establishment until his death in 1935. Clyde Smith would be the cashier, being responsible for the day-to-day operations. This institution remained an independent bank until 1975, when the Bank was sold to Jake Butcher's United American Bank of Knoxville, Tennessee.

All of these endeavors would lead to financial success for these businessmen and would influence the vocations of many of their nephews and their children. Many of our ancestors were active in the mercantile business during their lives, as this vocation became prominent in our family history.

The Stark-Phillips & Co. general store (circa 1900)

Chapter 8
Henry Clay Nicks, Last of a Generation

Henry Clay Nicks was born on March 6, 1854, the third child and first son of Bart and America Nicks. There is little direct information available concerning his formative years. We know that his father resided in Montgomery County, Tennessee, in 1850 and that Bart had mortgaged property owned in Dickson County in 1855. Sometime between these two dates, Bart moved to Dickson County. There is little to support the exact location of Henry's birth, but he was born either in Stayton or moved there as a young boy.

Mr. Earl Schmittou states in his article on Stayton that Henry Clay was one of the early students in a log schoolhouse that was located close to the present location of the Friendship Church of Christ.[56] In the 1860 census his two older sisters are listed as having attended school, so we know that a school would have existed. In terms of his own children, Henry would place a high premium on the value of an education.

Henry Clay grew up during a very difficult time in Middle Tennessee. He would have been six years old at the beginning of the Civil War and almost twelve at its conclusion. The postwar and

Reconstruction years saw little advancement in the accessibility of goods and services. The economy in northern Dickson County remained based on agriculture, with the exception of the iron ore industry, which had begun to decline in Dickson County. The availability of capital for expansion and growth was almost non-existent. Most families would be dependent on what they could raise on the farm for their subsistence.

Henry's relationship with blacks would have been different from that of later generations, different even from what his younger siblings would know. He was eight years old when the Emancipation Proclamation was signed. He would be the last of a generation that knew slavery on a firsthand basis, and that generation never moderated their views on blacks.

The 1880 census lists a black 14-year-old female, by the name of Peggy Bell, living in the Henry Nicks household. She was a "housekeeper." Peggy Bell again appears in Henry's household in 1900, this time as a servant. She was then 34 years of age. Although not listed in census data, family members would also recall a black man named Charlie who lived and worked on the farm. Henry was of the generation that employed blacks that had gained their freedom after the Civil War.

It is a certainty, given the time and place of his youth, that Henry Clay grew up working on his father's farm. With the exception of the Cumberland Furnace, there were no other opportunities for employment. Being the oldest boy, he would have had responsibilities on the farm. We know he farmed his entire life, and all the evidence points to the fact that he was successful.

Bart Nicks had three sons that would attain adulthood, Henry, Frank and Warren. Only the youngest, Warren, would not farm for a living but would enter the field of merchandising. Henry was nine years older than Warren, but there seems to have been a generation of difference in how they led their lives.

On September 30, 1875, Henry Clay Nicks would marry Sophronia Rufus Matthews, daughter of Buckner Wynn and Sarah Coffee Weakley. The two families were neighbors; the Matthews lived on a large farm almost adjacent to the farm where Henry grew up. It appears that Henry married well.

Henry Clay and Sophronia Nicks

Absalom Doak Nicks Jr., who was Henry's uncle, would perform the ceremony. He was a gospel minister in the Church of Christ as well as a state representative. J. J. Hudgins witnessed the marriage. Mr. Hudgins was Henry's brother-in-law by virtue of his marriage to Henry's oldest sister, Mary. Sophronia was 40 days short of her 18th birthday when they were married, and Henry had reached his 21st birthday.

Sophronia was the youngest of the Matthews children. She had an older brother, Anthony A. (1848–1912), and an older sister, Jane Western (1851–1929). Jane would marry Cave Johnson

Phillips, and the sisters would live next door for most of their married lives. The children of Jane and Cave Johnson Phillips would marry into the Nicks family.

Buckner Matthews was born in Lunenburg County, Virginia, and had moved to Montgomery County, Tennessee, as a boy. He was known throughout the area as "Buck." Most of the land that Henry would farm had been acquired from Mr. Matthews.

During Henry Clay's early life and throughout the remainder of the century, the population of Stayton would increase. However, the geographical boundaries and the mobility of its residents would change very little. This aspect of life was not unique to Stayton but was experienced in most rural areas of the South. Families with 8 to 10 children were common, for the simple reason that families required the labor to sustain self-sufficient family units and infant-mortality rates were, compared to later times, relatively high.

This circumstance led to large family units living in close proximity to one another, providing most of the social interaction. The size of these families resulted in a larger range of ages among siblings than what we are accustomed to today. Nineteen years separated the ages of Henry's oldest sister, Mary, and his youngest brother, Stephen.

The result of all this was marriages often occurring between brothers and sisters of neighboring families. Families related to our own ancestor through marriage include the Starks, Phillips, McCaslin and Harris families in the Stayton area. The limited mobility of the population also resulted in many business partnerships being formed within families.

Buckner Wynn Matthews (ca. 1895)

Sophronia Nicks and Jane Phillips,
Daughters of Buck Matthews (ca. 1922)

78

The 1880 census states who Henry and Sophronia's neighbors were and provides insight into the close proximity of certain families. Living adjacent to, or in close proximity with, one another at this time were the Thomas Stark family, the Henry Nicks family, the Ben T. McCaslin family, the Bart and America Nicks family and Bart's oldest daughter, Mary (Nicks) Hudgins, who by that time was widowed. Mr. Stark had a son, Elijah Washington Stark, who would later marry Henry's youngest sister, Florence. Ben T. McCaslin was Henry's brother-in-law having married Henry's older sister, Martha, in 1866.

Farther down the road lived Buckner Matthews, who was Sophronia's father. Adjacent to this household lived Cave Phillips, who had married Jane Matthews, Buck Matthews's other daughter. Cave and Jane had a son, Rufus Slayden, who in 1904 would marry Ben T. McCaslin's youngest daughter, Florence Eudora McCaslin. Cave and Jane Phillips also had a daughter, Dottie, who in 1897 would marry B. W. S. Nicks Jr. This marriage would have made Dottie both the niece and sister-in-law of Sophronia Nicks.

Following are some impressions of Henry that I have formed through memories that my uncles shared with me. He was a strict disciplinarian who was all business and believed in hard work. They remembered sitting in his lap and that he smelled of tobacco because he smoked a pipe. He was the song leader at the Friendship Church of Christ, even though he could not "carry a tune in a bucket."

At the division of Henry's assets following his death, no mention is made of any motorized vehicles. There was, however, a horse and buggy. It is probable that he never owned or drove an automobile.

My Dad remembered his Grandmother as being a very kind and loving person who was a wonderful cook. It was said that she made the very best teacakes and would keep them in a kettle beside the fireplace. Large portions of her fried chicken were always served at Sunday dinners. Grand Ma had a fox horn made from the horn of a cow that has been handed down through the family. She would use it to call the men in from the fields instead of using a dinner bell. My Dad gave that fox horn to me.

Records do not provide any evidence that Henry was ever involved in a partnership with anyone. At a time when commerce was increasing locally, he seems to have steered his own ship. The land he bought was singularly owned, and he seems to have farmed only his own land. The same can be said of his brother, Frank. These two brothers stood in contrast, in that respect, to their younger brother, Warren.

As stated earlier, the 1890 census was lost due to a fire. During the period between 1880 and 1900, we have little information on the movement and activity of our families. Since my grandfather, B. C. Nicks, was born in 1881, the first census record of him appears in 1900, when he was 19 years old. Buck Matthews and B. W. S. Nicks, my great-great grandfathers, passed away in the mid-1890s, their last mention occurring in the census of 1880.

At some point after 1875, Henry and Sophronia purchased a portion of her father's farm and built the house where they would remain for the rest of their lives. The home still stands, a large two-story structure in a style that was prevalent at the time called an "H house" because of its floor plan.

The house featured a large covered front porch across the front. The original front porch was removed in the 1960s in favor of a smaller one. As the family grew, additions were made by adding more bedrooms and enlarging the kitchen.

The house was located on a large farm of at least 250 acres. Facing the house and to the left was located a cave, which had a spring flowing from it. The entrance to the cave was framed with

Henry and Sophronia Nicks Home, ca. 2003

Pecan Tree at H. C. Nicks Home
This was thought to be the largest tree in Tennessee at the time.
ca. 1922 - Ladies in this picture are unknown.

81

stone, and a door was placed there that allowed the family to use it as a springhouse. Milk, butter, eggs and other perishables were stored there as well as watermelons in season. My Dad told me that a water line was installed that would bring running water into the house by gravity.

To the right of the house, there stood a giant pecan tree. It was thought to be between 150 and 200 years old and was said to be the largest living tree in Middle Tennessee. It measured 27 feet in circumference, and one limb measured 90 feet in length.[57] This tree was destroyed by a storm in 1973.

Family of Henry Clay and Sophronia Nicks

Seated Front Row, L-R: Barton Nicks (11 yrs.), Emmett Nicks (6 yrs.), Evie Nicks (8 yrs.), Speight Nicks (4 yrs.), Buckner Clay Nicks (14 yrs.)
Seated Back Row, L-R: Henry Clay Nicks (41 yrs.), Sophronia Matthews Nicks (38 yrs.) Euvella Nicks (11 mos.), Buckner Matthews (84)
Girls Standing, L-R: Lena Nicks (16 yrs.) and Agnes Nicks (19 yrs.)
Man standing behind Agnes to the right – Elijah Washington Daniel (27 yrs.)

A family portrait was taken sometime in 1895. The date can be approximated by considering the clues offered in the picture. The baby in Sophronia's lap is Euvella Nicks, born on September 27, 1894. This would make her 10 to 11 months old in the picture. Buck Matthews had died in March of 1896; his wife, Sara Weakley Matthews, died on August 15, 1895 and is not present in the picture. The picture was obviously taken during warm weather since both Emmett and Speight are wearing short pants and Euvella is barefooted. Taking into consideration the black dresses that Sophronia and Evie are wearing and the suits that the men are wearing, it is possible that the picture was taken in conjunction with the funeral of Buck's wife on August 15, 1895.

It is interesting to note the difference in the size and physical maturity of Bart Nicks seated on the far left and B.C. seated on the far right. Only three years and two months separated their ages, but a far greater difference in size suggests a disparity in health and development. Bart was sick most of his life and would pass away in 1904, before his 20th birthday.

The man on the porch to the far right is believed to be E. W. Daniel, who would later marry Agnes Nicks in December of 1901. This image of E. W. Daniel favors another likeness of him in a photo that was taken in 1907.

I acquired this picture from Albert Nicks who had displayed it at Nicks Hardware in Dickson. The names were noted on the back of the picture.

At the time of the 1900 census Henry Clay and Sophronia were living with all 10 of their children. It is interesting to note that the oldest child, Agnes, was 23 years of age and the youngest, Dewey, was 1. None of the children was married at that time. The family resided at the same house where the family photographs were made in 1895. They were living next door to Sophronia's sister, Jane Phillips, and her husband, Cave. These two properties would make up the original Buck Matthews farm and was probably purchased by the daughters sometime before his death.

Henry Clay raised various crops and livestock but was principally engaged in the tobacco business. He not only raised a tobacco crop on his farm but was also in the business of buying tobacco from other farmers in the area. The harvested crop would be "prized" and prepared for shipping to Clarksville, where the "fired" leaf would then be sold to the tobacco-product manufacturers.

His business was called the Tobacco Factory & Warehouse. This warehouse was located on a large parcel of land that was adjacent to his house. The building was originally built as a barn, and an addition was added in 1911. Parts of the foundation of this structure can still be found in this field.

In his article about early life and business in Stayton, Mr. Earl Schmittou stated that "Henry Clay Nicks prized tobacco at his warehouse and shipped it to Clarksville, Tennessee, for the Tobacco Protective Association."[58] "Prizing" is the process of packing the tobacco leaf, after it has been "fired" and stripped from the stalk, into large wooden barrels suitable for shipping to the buyers of the leaf, who would then process the tobacco into a product suitable for use by the consumer.

The Tobacco Protective Association was a large group of tobacco farmers in southern Kentucky and northern Middle Tennessee who attempted to organize for collectively bargaining with the large tobacco companies in an effort to increase the market price of their tobacco.

These organizing efforts occurred between 1904 and 1910 and were directed toward dealing with a monopoly that had been created by the American Tobacco Company of North Carolina. These efforts led to much violence and bloodshed that has been referred to as the Tobacco Wars. The issue was resolved when on May 9, 1911, the United States Supreme Court ruled in United

States v. American Tobacco Co. that the Duke trust, ATC, was indeed a monopoly and was in violation of the Sherman Anti-Trust Act of 1890.[59]

In his book on the tobacco wars, *On Bended Knees*, Bill Cunningham extensively covers the history and issues regarding these conflicts between tobacco growers and the American Tobacco Company. No one engaged in the raising of tobacco was unaffected by those events, and growers were forced by economics either to take the side of the Protective Association or the American Tobacco Company. It would appear that Henry was on the side of the Protective Association.

Most of the activity and violence that was associated with this conflict occurred in northern Middle Tennessee and southern Kentucky. The violence that is associated with this period came no closer to Stayton than Clarksville, Tennessee.

There are no records of any of these activities taking place in Dickson County, but Henry would have been aware of them since his warehouse was operated for the benefit of the Protective Association.

As discussed earlier, Henry Clay attended school in a log schoolhouse that was located in the general area of the Friendship Church of Christ. B. C. Nicks also attended school there for his early education and most likely was taught by his aunt, Mary Hudgins.

A new school was built around 1899 and was located closer to the "business district." The school was known as Stayton School and appears to have provided education for grades 1–12.

A photograph of the student body in 1908 provides some insight as to the early education of Henry's children. Included in the photo are Emmett (age 19), Speight (age 17), Euvalla (age 14), Albert (age 11) and Dewey (age 9). All of Henry and Sophronia's children that were of school age were present. Evie, B.C., Lena and

Agnes were older and had finished this portion of their education. Rosa Powell Speight is also in this photograph.

The new school consisted of an auditorium and four classrooms. An upstairs room was provided for teaching band, and Slayden Phillips was the instructor. Penmanship was also taught, and students came from a wide area to attend. Some of these students boarded in the home of Warren Nicks.[60]

As stated before, B. C. Nicks would continue his education at Southside Preparatory School in Southside, Tennessee. In today's educational structure, this school would have provided educational opportunities somewhere between high school and college. The curriculum offered included studies in algebra, geometry, economics, Greek, Latin, composition, penmanship and all of the sciences.[61] The school was known throughout the area as providing a practical yet classical education.

Isham Harper, who was Kate Nicks's brother-in-law, was the head master at this school for several years. In 1907 the school decided to construct a new building, and the land was donated by H. C. Lyle and Albert Hudgins.[62] H. C. Lyle was Kate's older brother. and Albert Hudgins was B.C.'s first cousin.

Not only would Henry and Sophronia provide B.C. with an opportunity to further his education; the three youngest boys were sent to a boarding school in Huntington, Tennessee, to continue their education. Indicative of the times, there is no record of any of the girls being afforded this opportunity. There is also no record that Emmett attended any schools beyond Stayton. At age 20 Emmett is listed in the 1910 census as working on the farm with his father.

Southern Normal School (aka the Industrial and Training School of Huntington) operated in Huntington, Tennessee. Speight, Albert and Dewey all attended school at Southern Normal. The boys would have taken a train from Cumberland Furnace to Pond Switch on the Mineral Line and then would ride the L&N line to Huntington. The total trip was about eighty miles. They would have boarded at the school; it is not known how often they would have come home or how long the academic year lasted. Both Speight and Dewey would later attend college and then Pharmacy School.

Henry and Sophronia's commitment to their children's education is remarkable considering the standards of the day. There was no precedent at that time that would have guided them. It is notable that Henry seems to be the only child of his family that afforded this opportunity to his children. It speaks to their financial standing as well as their understanding of the importance of an education. It also shows an insight into a future where more would be required to be successful. While Henry chose farming as the occupation he would follow, he and Sophronia wanted something different for their children. It also speaks to the values held by Sophronia and her influence on what was best for her children. The mothers of our Nicks family contributed greatly to their family's successes.

The family attended the Friendship Church of Christ. It may have been known as a Christian Church at the time, continuing a family tradition in this faith. The property where the Friendship Church is located was donated by Henry's father, B.W.S.

The census of 1900 is the last record of Henry and Sophronia's entire family living in the same household. The decade would provide times of joy and moments of sadness, as many changes would occur during the ensuing ten years.

In December of 1901 their oldest daughter, Agnes, married Elijah Washington Daniel, and they would have their first child, William Nicks Daniel, in 1905. This would be Henry and Sophronia's first grandchild. Agnes would give birth to their second child, Howard, in 1907.

In April of 1902, Henry and Sophronia's second daughter, Lena, would marry Robert Martin Nicks, who was her third cousin.

In 1903, B.C. would move to Nashville to live with his mother's brother, Anthony Matthews, and work in Anthony's wholesale grocery business. In April of 1907, B.C. would marry Katherine Lyle, and they would begin housekeeping in Dull, Tennessee. In 1909, they would have their first child, a son named James Henry, the third grandchild of Henry and Sophronia.

In May of 1904, Henry and Sophronia suffered the loss of their 19-year-old son, Barton Rufus. Barton was their fourth child, and according to family history battled illness most of his life. He was buried in the Nicks/Speight Cemetery in Stayton.

After the death of her husband in 1894, America Agnes would live with her daughter Dora Speight and her husband Jack. The 1900 census shows America in that household with others, including her sister, Leah Nesbitt. On March 10, 1905, America would passed away at the age of 74. She is buried next to her husband, Bart, at the Nicks/Speight Cemetery in Stayton.

Henry would also lose two of his sisters in this decade. His oldest sister, Mary Hudgins, would pass away on June 22, 1903, at 54 years of age. There is no record as to the cause of her death because Tennessee did not require the issuance of death certificates until 1908. Mary had been widowed since 1877. She would have been living in Southside with her son, Albert. She was a teacher in Southside, Tennessee, and is buried there.

On February 23, 1909 at the age of 44, Henry's youngest sister, Florence Stark, would also pass away. Her death certificate states that she died of "heart trouble." Her youngest child, Clifford Stark, would become a college professor in the study of agriculture. The Stark Agribusiness and Agriscience Center on the M.T.S.U. campus in Murfreesboro is named in his honor.

This decade included the marriage of three of Henry and Sophronia's children, the birth of their first three grandchildren and the loss of his mother and two of his sisters. When the first decade of the 20th century closed, Henry had reached his 55th birthday, and Sophronia was 52 years of age.

The 1910 Census was taken at Stayton on May 4, 1910. The Nickses were living at the same place. Some of the neighbors had changed, but Sophronia's sister, Jane, and her husband, Cave, still lived one door down. A few miles west on Stayton Road lived Henry's brother, Frank.

Henry's children who still lived at home were Evie, 23 years old, Emmett, 20 years of age, Speight, 18 years old, Euvella, 15 years old, Albert, 13 years old, and Dewey was 11 years of age. The census also lists in the household a 28-year-old single, white male by the name of Walter Garrett, and his relationship to the family is listed as a hired man.

All of the boys except Albert are listed as working on the farm, as is Mr. Garrett. There is nothing listed for Albert in the space provided for occupation, and he may well have been away at school.

Evie would marry Dan Harris in 1910, Euvella would marry John Calvin Weems in September of 1914 and Emmett would marry Mary Larkins in December of 1914.

To Henry and Sophronia would be born 20 grandchildren. As previously mentioned, three would be born before 1910. Nine of their grandchildren were born between 1910 and 1920. Bob, Carney and Lyle would be born to B.C. and Kate. Allen Elijah and Rufus were born to Agnes and E. W. Daniel, Margaret was born to Dan and Evie Harris, and Sarah was born to Emmett and Mary. Also, Sophronia and Joe A. were born to Euvella and John Weems.

Henry and Sophronia would lose only one grandchild during their lifetime, when on March 16, 1917, Allen Elijah Daniel died from pneumonia that developed as he was recovering from the measles. He was 6 years old and attended school at the time.

89

In 1916 Sophronia's brother-in-law, Cave Phillips, would pass away, and her sister Jane continued to live next door in the household of her son, Ray, and his family.

During this decade Speight, Albert and Dewey gained their education. As stated earlier, all three of the boys attended high school in Huntingdon. This fact is mentioned in Speight's biographical information included in his U. T. Pharmacy School yearbook, and Albert's family has his diploma.

During the latter part of the decade, the United States would enter World War I and all of Henry's boys would register for the draft in either 1917 or 1918. Albert and Speight served in the military during this period. These draft registrations state that Speight, Albert and Dewey were all working at home on the family farm. According to their statements, B.C. and Emmett were both merchants in the Nicks Brothers General Mercantile store, which was located in the White Oak Flat community. More will be written on this partnership under B. C. Nicks's chapter.

By 1920 Henry would have been 66 years of age, and Sophronia would have turned 63 in November. All of their children had left home by that time, with the exception of Albert, who is listed in their household as a farm laborer in the 1920 census.

By 1920 Agnes and E. W. Daniel had moved to Dickson; Emmett and B. C. were living four houses apart in White Oak Flat, listing their occupation as farmers. Speight was in his next-to-last year of pharmacy school, and Albert was still single and living at home. I have found no records that account for Dewey in 1920, but at the age of 21 he was most likely in Memphis attending school. All of the daughters had married and had begun families of their own.

Later in 1920 Emmett moved to Murfreesboro to a farm that he and B.C. had purchased. B.C. would eventually move his family to Dickson. Albert would marry Myrtice Fussell in 1922, and they would reside with her parents on Jones Creek Road in Dickson where he would farm with his father-in-law, Sam Fussell. Lena and Robert were living in Nashville where he was a machinist. Evie and Dan lived in Charlotte where he was the Postmaster. Euvella and John Weems were residing in the Southside area, where he farmed.

In 1925 Henry would lose a third sister, Eudora Speight. Her death certificate states that she "died before medical attention could reach her." She was said to suffer from "high blood pressure." The doctor who signed the death certificate was a local physician who was well known in area, Dr. Cunningham.

Another of Henry's siblings would pass away on September 28, 1927, his brother Frank, who was 69 years old. Frank's death certificate states that his cause of death was "paralysis complicated by hypostatic pneumonia." The attending physician was, again, Dr. Cunningham. Frank Nicks was a farmer all of his life. Dr. Cunningham was married to Frank's daughter, Eula Agnes Nicks.

Six months prior to Frank Nicks's death, on March 31, 1927, Henry and Sophronia would sit down with family members and execute a plan for their long-term care. This legal document is titled as a contract and is recorded in the Register's Office of Dickson County. The sophistication of this plan and how it avoided conflict in the family is notable. The language and terminology used would suffice in today's world.

The agreement first states that Henry and Sophronia were the parents of Emmett and the parents of "several other" children that were grown, married and had moved away from home. The document then states that both parents were now "past middle age." It continues with the fact that Emmett was living in their house with them and was cultivating their farm. Emmett was married and had two children.

The parents then explain their purpose. "The parents are now desirous of securing assurance of support, maintenance and care during their remaining years and they believe that their son Emmett is a suitable person to assure them this support, maintenance and care." The parties then agree to the following terms:

First, Emmett agrees to reside with his parents and provide their needed support. Then they proceed to define maintenance and support to be "in accordance with their present social standing and their past custom, to include doctor's bills and medical bills."

Second, in addition to the support outlined in the first part of the agreement, Emmett agrees to provide Henry and Sophronia $100 per year for spending money. This support is to be made in quarterly payments and continue to be paid to the survivor in the event of the death of either party.

Third, Emmett agrees to bear all the expenses of upkeep of the farm and home, including taxes and insurance. In consideration for Emmett rendering these services, they agree to the following. First, Emmett shall have full control of the proceeds from the farm, free from rent or other claims. Second, after the death of both parents, Emmett is to be paid $400 for each year that he complies with the terms of the agreement, including $400 for any partial year. These monies are to be paid out of the estate after all funeral bills and any other just debts are paid. Third, the remainder of the estate is to be divided equally among all the children or their heirs according to law, including Emmett.

Henry and Sophronia retained all rights and control over their personal property, not including the farm machinery and tools necessary to a farming operation.

Then, to guarantee that Emmett was secure in collecting his money because of the care that he was to provide, Henry and Sophronia placed a mortgage on the farm in favor of Emmett. If there was no money left to pay Emmett upon their death, the farm was to be sold under foreclosure and the proceeds first used to pay Emmett any sums he might be due. They named their oldest son, B. C. Nicks, as the trustee of this mortgage.

The document then proceeds to describe the tracts that they owned and that comprise the farm. This section sheds light on how and from whom they obtained the farm. It came from several tracts that all appear to have been purchased from various parties. It specifically says that part of the property was purchased from Buck Matthews. This would confirm how the Matthews property was acquired and that it was not by gift or inheritance. The family picture of 1895 has Buck Matthews sitting on the porch with the rest of Henry's family. His wife was deceased. It is possible that the property transferred at his death in exchange for long-term care, much in the same manner that Henry and Sophronia were proposing in 1927. If so, that would explain where they got the template for the transaction they executed.

The remainder of the document contains various legal provisions that would protect all parties and insure that the document was legal.

Almost a year later, on March 4, 1928, Henry would pass away after being ill since February 26. His wife, Sophronia, would pass away only a month later, on April 6, 1928, after being under the care of a physician since Henry's death. His death certificate states that he died of influenza complicated by encephalitis and double branch pneumonia. Her death certificate shows she also died from influenza complicated by facial encephalitis and double branch pneumonia. They died of the same thing. The term "facial" is included in Sophronia's diagnosis and not included in Henry's diagnosis. One of the symptoms of encephalitis is the swelling of the facial tissues.

These death certificates confirm a story told to me by my father. Dr. Cunningham was the community doctor in Stayton at the time and was married to Henry's niece. He had been their doctor for a long time. B.C. was not satisfied that his parents were receiving the care that they needed and sought out a second opinion. Dr. R. P. Beasley was a physician practicing in Dickson and a good friend of our family. B.C. asked Dr. Beasley if he would consult with Dr. Cunningham and provide a second opinion. After the visit, Dr. Beasley agreed with the diagnosis and treatment. The death certificates are signed by both Dr. Beasley and Dr. Cunningham.

The information on Henry's death certificate was provided by Eula Nicks Cunningham. She was a niece, being the daughter of Frank Nicks, and was married to Dr. Cunningham. The information given on Sophronia's death certificate was provided by Dottye Nicks (Mrs. Warren Nicks). She was Sophronia's niece and sister-in-law. Sophronia's name on the death certificate is listed as Fronia Nicks, which may indicate what her friends and family would have called her.

Their burial would be the first since the passing of B. W. S. Nicks wherein a family member was not buried in the Nicks-Speight Cemetery in Stayton. Henry and Sophronia were buried in Union Cemetery in Dickson. Records of Union Cemetery indicate that the grave plots in which Henry and Sophronia were buried belonged to Boyd Nicks.

Boyd Nicks was the son of Henry's first cousin, Alexander Campbell Nicks. Boyd would have been 37 years old at the time of Henry's passing and lived in Nashville, where he operated a restaurant named the Eat-A-Bite Café. Whether the gravesites were purchased or received as a gift is not known. It is somewhat common to see cemetery deeds that have never been recorded.

My Dad recalled that his Grandfather had stated that he wanted to be buried in Dickson. He said that he did not believe the younger generation would take care of the rural family cemeteries. He was right; the Nicks Cemetery is in bad repair today.

Emmett Nicks and his wife, Mary, are also buried in the same area, as are their two daughters. Emmett is named as the owner of those plots.

After the deaths of their parents, the children began settling their parent's affairs. On December 21, 1928, all of the children signed a deed transferring the farm to Emmett. The children state that they had agreed on the value of the property and all farm machinery and tools to be $6,000. There are nine children surviving making each child's part $666.66. The children all agreed that Emmett should be the purchaser. It is further stated that a horse and buggy were still on the farm and that they should be included in the transfer.

This deed provides us with information as to the location of all the children in 1929. The signatures of the children were required to be notarized, and this action tells us where they lived in 1928. The signatures of Buckner Clay, Agnes Daniel, Euvalla Weems and Albert Nicks were notarized in Dickson. Lena Nicks's and Evie Harris' signatures were notarized in Nashville. Speight Nicks's affirmation took place in Memphis, while Dewey Nicks's took place in El Paso, Texas.

Henry and Sophronia were born into the Civil War and lived their lives during the period of Reconstruction that saw many changes in their world. They not only survived; they prospered. They had raised their children in a manner that prepared them to meet even greater challenges. They were truly the last of a generation who were self-sufficient, affected mainly by events in their own community.

Chapter 9
Children of Change

Henry Clay and Sophronia Nicks had ten children, born from 1876 to 1899, a period of almost 28 years. There would be 4 girls and 6 boys, and all would survive to adulthood with the exception of Barton Rufus, who would die at the age of 19 years, 6 months.

Daughters of H. C. and Sophronia Nicks
L-R, Lena Nicks, Agnes Daniel, Evie Nicks and Euvella Weems

The first child was a daughter, Sarah Agnes, who was born on September 18, 1876. Agnes would marry Elijah Washington Daniel on December 26, 1901, when she was 21 years old. Elijah Washington Daniel was born on October 24, 1868. He was eight years older than Agnes and was known as Lidge. When B.C. and Kate married, they first shared a house with the Daniels and would be partners in a small country store known as Daniel & Nicks. E.W. and Agnes would move to Dickson about 1910, and over the next 20 years he would manage Dickson Wholesale Grocery. He served as a director in the First National Bank in Dickson from 1921 until 1933[63] and as an Elder in the Walnut Street Church of Christ.[64]

The Daniels had four sons, William Nicks (1904–1965), Howard Lyle (1907–1951), Allen Elijah (1911–1917) and Rufus Weakly (1915–1955). Their third child, Allen Elijah, would perish from pneumonia that was brought on as a complication of the measles. He died when he was six years of age.

Their oldest child, William, attended Oakmont School in Dickson for his early education. During his high school years, he was a student at Gallatin Private Institute, in Gallatin, Tennessee. He attended college at Vanderbilt University where he played football and graduated with a degree in engineering. He would marry Pauline Nicks in June of 1931. Pauline was a daughter of Tolbert Fanning Nicks Jr. She descended from Perry Nicks, Bart's older brother, and was a fifth cousin to William.

Their second son was named Howard Lyle Daniel. Mention of his birth was made in the Kate Nicks diary of 1907. There can be little doubt that his middle name was taken from Kate's maiden name. The 1928 Vanderbilt yearbook lists him as student in the sophomore class. According to census records, he did not graduate.

97

Howard would be the original owner of City Service Dry Cleaners, then located on South Main Street in Dickson. Sometime between 1931 and 1934 this business would be closed by the County for failure to pay taxes. Bob Nicks provided me with the details involving the transfer of ownership of this business.

The building had been padlocked by the Sheriff under orders from the County. Bob was then living at home. Many friends of our family soon realized that the clothing they had left at the cleaners was now locked up in the building. B.C. obtained a key to the building and the delivery truck. He asked Bob to go to the store, gather the items of clothing belonging to customers and deliver them. As Bob made the deliveries, the customers began to give him other items to take back and dry-clean for them. He received enough of this "new" business to reopen the store. That began Bob's career in the dry cleaning business.

After a time, Bob had saved enough money to pay the back taxes and to purchase the delivery truck from First National Bank, which had repossessed it.

After several months of operation, Bob was approached by E. W. Daniel in the lobby of First National Bank. Mr. Daniel stated that he felt the business belonged to Howard and that he was not going to let Bob "run over them." Bob replied, "I'm not going to let you run over me, either."

Bob Nicks related that after that confrontation, Mr. Daniel sent Pauline Daniel, William's wife, to the store to observe the operation and to assist Bob if necessary. Bob said that after a few days, Pauline told him that she did not think what Mr. Daniel was doing was right, and she did not return. After a few years, Bob moved the business to North Main Street where he successfully operated it until the late 1960s.

In 1935 Howard would marry Nell Taylor, and in 1936 they would have a son, Joe Howard. By 1940 they had divorced and Howard was living in Dyersburg, Tennessee, working as an insurance salesman. From February of 1942 until September of 1945, Howard would serve in the Army Air Corps. At the time of his death in 1951, he was a part-time mail clerk at the Post Office in Dickson.

Rufus was their youngest son. I have found no information regarding his secondary education, but he attended college for four years, graduating from Harding University in Searcy, Arkansas. Records also show that he had attended David Lipscomb College. At that time, Lipscomb was a two-year institution, and he most likely finished his degree at Harding. The 1940 census has Rufus and his wife, Myrtle, living in his older brother's (William's) household in Nashville. Rufus and Myrtle would later divorce. This record also specifies that he was a salesman. At his death in 1955, he was a carpenter working construction jobs.

At least two of these sons would commit suicide. Howard would be the first in 1951 at the age of 44, then William, in 1965, at the age of 61. There is conflicting information regarding Rufus.

The family history that I have been told was that each of the three boys took his life. My Dad and Rufus were close friends in their younger years, and my Dad never agreed with those who believed Rufus had committed suicide. Rufus's death certificate states that he died at his home of myocardial failure and that death was instant. There is a section provided on the death certificate to be marked by the attending physician if the death was by suicide. This box was left blank on Rufus's certificate. The obituary that ran in the *Tennessean* the following day states that he died at his home of a heart attack. His brothers had died from self-inflected gunshot wounds. If Rufus's death was anything other than by natural causes, there is no evidence that he died from a gunshot wound.

Whatever the cause, all three deaths were tragic losses of men who were in their prime. How does one explain such a tragedy? Of course, the best answer to the predictable "Why?" is,

"I don't know." None of us can answer such a question, whether the suicide in question exists within or without our own families. However, we can offer a few observations. Just as economic, religious and political dynamics have evolved over the generations of our family's history, so also has our understanding and treatment of the kind of depression that is suffered by one who elects self-destruction. In earlier times, a suicide was considered a shameful act, a terrible weakness of character and a blight on a family history. Today, we have the benefit of counselors with the social and medical training to address these issues before they happen. We know that medications, together with trained counseling, can prevent such tragedies. We also know that genetic tendencies play a role in the decisions of those who choose this dreadful option. All we can say, with certainty, about Lidge and Agnes's adult sons is that at least two died by their own hand, and we can only imagine the burden of their family's pain.

Elijah Washington would pass away on October 24, 1934, from paralysis that resulted from a stroke. Dr. R. P. Beasley stated on the death certificate that high blood pressure was the contributing factor. On December 27, 1954, Agnes would die from uremia, complicated by severe generalized arteriosclerosis. At the time of her death, she was residing in Bennett Nursing Home in Nashville. Both are buried in Union Cemetery.

On March 6, 1879, a second child was born to Henry and Sophronia, a daughter who was named Lena Eudora. On April 16, 1902, at the age of 23, she would marry Robert Martin Nicks.

Robert and Len would have no children. They would spend most of their married life in Nashville, on Nevada Avenue. The 1940 census data shows that Bob was an auto mechanic.

Children of Henry Clay Nicks and Sophronia Nicks
L-R Speight Nicks, B. C. Nicks, Agnes Daniel, Lena Nicks, Dewey Nicks, Euvella
Weems, Evie Harris, Albert Nicks, Emmett Nicks, ca. 1935

Spouses of Henry Clay's Children
L-R Dan Harris, John Weems, Robert Martin Nicks, Kate Lyle Nicks, Mary Larkins
Nicks, Myrtice Fussell Nicks, Vera Nicks and Hazel Nicks, ca. 1935

According to that census, Bob owned his own shop and Lena was his bookkeeper. He was the son of William Asbury Nicks and a grandson of Perry Nicks. Bob and Lena would have been third cousins. Census data as early as 1920 indicates that Bob's mother, Margaret Ann, lived with them. His father died in 1899 and was buried at the Rock Church of Christ on Jones Creek, Dickson.Bob was likely raised in the Jones Creek area, and his parents ran the County Farm for a period. As we will see later, Lena's younger brother, Buckner Clay, lived with them on Nevada Avenue in 1906 while working in Nashville.

Bob and Lena would spend their life in Nashville. He passed away on June 23, 1961 and she would die on September 28, 1972. They are buried in the Union Cemetery in Dickson, in the plot of her parents.

Henry and Sophronia's first son, Buckner Clay Nicks, was born on August 16, 1881. He was named after his grandfather, Buckner Wynn Matthews and his father, Henry Clay. His life is detailed in the following chapter.

Buckner Clay would be known as B.C., as B. or simply as B without any period. More often than not I have referred to him as B.C., to avoid the confusion that a single initial can provoke in a text, with or without the period, but in all cases, the person being discussed is Buckner Clay Nicks, my grandfather.

Barton Rufus Nicks was born on October 13, 1884. He is the fourth child and second son born to Henry and Sophronia. Barton would pass away 5 months before his 20th birthday on May 31, 1904. He was 3½ years younger than B.C. My father said that Bart had battled illness most of his life and was small for his age. In the 1900 census both Bart and B.C. were in Henry Clay's household, their occupations listed as "farm laborer." The family picture of 1895 shows Bart and B.C. sitting on the steps of the home place. The difference in their size is noticeable given there were only 3½ years difference in age. Bart is buried in the Nicks family cemetery in Stayton.

Barton Rufus Nicks

On June 3, 1887, the fifth child in less than 11 years was born to the family. Her name was Evie Jane Nicks, and she would marry Dan Harris on October 6, 1910, when she was 23 years old. Daniel Heard Harris was born on March 22, 1886, and was the son of Thomas Wetherstone Harris and Sarah Ann Heard. Dan's brother, George Harris, would marry Warren Nicks's daughter and much later would own and operate the Speight/Nicks General Store. Dan also had a brother, Bob, who was the father of Mary Ann Self.

Dan Harris served as postmaster at Charlotte, Tennessee, and lived there in 1920. In 1922, the couple moved to Nashville and lived on Nevada Avenue, the same street where Evie's older sister, Lena, lived. Dan worked at the Post Office in Nashville. They lived at the same address in 1940, and Dan was listed as a supervisor with the Post Office.

This couple had two daughters, Margaret Weakly Harris, who married Allan Little, and Mary Agnes Harris, who married Paul Boyce. Agnes would have no children. Margaret and Allan Little had three children, two sons who died in infancy, and a daughter, Jane, who was born in 1955. Jane was mentally and physically handicapped. Margaret and Allan would spend most of their adult life providing care for their daughter.

Like his father-in-law, Allan spent his working career in the Nashville Post Office as a supervisor. Allan and Margaret were good friends of our family. Allan passed away in January of 2016. Margaret passed away on August 26, 2016, at the age of 101.

Henry Clay and Sophronia had their sixth child on August 12, 1889, a son. His given name was Charlie Emmett Nicks, and he married Mary Palestine Larkins, the daughter of J. A. and Mollie Larkins on December 31, 1914. She was a sister to Dobson and Calvin Larkins. They were married in her parents' home, and B. C. and Kate Nicks were witnesses to this marriage. (This is according to family records of the Larkins family.) Mary Larkins was born on March 1, 1895, which would have made her 19 years of age when they married.

Emmett Nicks would spend his life in the mercantile and farming business. During his younger years he would be a partner with his older brother, Buckner Clay. According to the 1920 census, he was living four doors down from B.C.'s family in the White Oak Flat community. These brothers would be partners in a general store in White Oak Flat named Nicks Brothers and were later in partnership on a large farm outside of Murfreesboro, Tennessee. Emmett and Mary would reside in Murfreesboro on this farm until 1926.

After his parents passed away in 1928, Emmett purchased the family farm in Stayton from his siblings. He would live and work on the farm until 1948. The 1940 census has him living at the home place in Stayton. When he sold the farm, he moved to Dickson and worked with his younger brother, Albert, at Nicks Hardware.

Emmett and Mary had two daughters, Sara Louise, who married Robert Elliott, and Claytie, who would marry Edward King Raymond. Claytie had three children: Billy, Martha King and Ted.

Emmett would pass away on May 10, 1962, and Mary would die on August 6, 1969. They are both buried at Union Cemetery in Dickson in a plot next to his father and mother.

Twenty-Five months after the birth of Emmett, Jack Speight Nicks would be born on October 4, 1891. He was the seventh child and fourth son to be born to Henry and Sophronia. He was named after his Aunt Dora's husband, John M. (Jack) Speight.

When he was 33 years of age, he would marry Verda Talley on June 5, 1924. Verda was born in Louisiana on November 27, 1894. She was 27 years old when they married, and I have found no records regarding where they wed. Speight and Verda would have no children.

Youngest Sons of H. C. and Sophronia Nicks
Speight, Albert and Dewey Nicks, circa 1978

According to the 1910 census, Speight was living at his father's home place in Stayton. He was farming with his father and older brother, Emmett. He registered for the draft on June 5, 1917, and stated in that document that he was home working for his father.

In the 1920 census, at the age of 28, he was single and boarding on South Orleans Street in Memphis. He was a student of pharmacy at the University of Tennessee. Speight Nicks was the first of many in our family who became Pharmacists. I have no information as to what would have influenced him to enter this profession, but he most certainly had an influence on others in our family.

In the 1921 U.T. Medical School yearbook, Speight is shown as a member of the senior class of the Pharmacy School. His biographical sketch states that he was a graduate of the Industrial and Training School in Huntington, Tennessee, and that he attended Valparaiso College in Valparaiso, Indiana, from 1916 through 1918. He attended U.T. Memphis from 1919 through 1921 and served two years in the Medical Department of the U.S. Army. The following is a quote from his yearbook: "His quiet, unassuming dignity and persistent 'A's' have won the admiration of all. We feel sure he will be a big success." He would have been 30 years old when he graduated from Pharmacy School.

In the 1930 census he was married and living on Fountain Court in Memphis. He was the owner of a pharmacy named Get Well Drug Store. James Nicks, his nephew, would board with and work for Speight while attending pharmacy school. A 1954 Memphis city directory lists the couple as living on Kimball Place, Memphis. Speight Nicks would die on January 14, 1980, and Vera would follow on April 4, 1981. They are buried in Memphis.

Birdie Euvella Nicks was the eighth child and youngest daughter in this family. She was born on September 27, 1894, and would marry John Calvin Weems on September 10, 1914. This was the second child of Henry and Sophronia to marry in 1914; their son Emmett had been married the previous month.

John Calvin Weems was born on April 18, 1893, and was raised in Montgomery County. His home was in the Rye's Chapel area, near Gallon Road and the Southside Road. Some references state that the Weems Family was from Southside.

Birdie and John's marriage produced seven children, 5 girls and 2 boys. I do not have much information on this family but did know their youngest son, a twin named Albert John Weems. He was an electrical inspector for several of the power companies in the area.

Euvella passed away on June 7, 1970, and John followed some 6 years later, on April 3, 1976. Both are buried at Rye's Chapel Cemetery in Montgomery County, Tennessee.

Anthony Albert Nicks was born on March 8, 1897, Henry and Sophronia's ninth child. He was named for his Uncle Anthony Amariah Matthews, his mother's older brother. Anthony Matthews was the owner of a wholesale grocery company in Nashville. The name Albert was taken from Albert Hudgins, his first cousin and the oldest son of Mary R. Nicks Hudgins. (Albert Hudgins was 28 years older than Albert Nicks.)

On April 15, 1922, Albert would marry Lura Myrtice Fussell at her father's home on Jones Creek Road in Dickson, Tennessee. Her father and mother were Samuel Fussell and Jennie Ray, and their farm was located next to the Fairview Community Club, across the road from the present lime quarry owned by Vulcan Materials Company. This farm was later known as the Potter place. Albert and Myrtice owned Nicks Hardware on South Main Street that operated at that location from 1939 until its closure in 2016.

They had two children, Samuel Clay Nicks (9/7/1923–1/18/2004) and Reba Annette Nicks (2/6/1928–5/16/2002). Clay was married to Earlene Turner and they had two children, Samuel Turner Nicks, born 8/19/1962, and Margo, born 12/26/1964. Clay and his son Sam both worked at the hardware store. Margo is a pharmacist in Kentucky.

George Dewey Nicks was born on May 1, 1899, the tenth child born to Henry and Sophronia. Almost 23 years had passed since the birth of their first child.

On August 15, 1929, Dewey would marry Hazel Edith Jones in El Paso, Texas. She was born on May 29, 1904. The 1930 census states that they were living in El Paso. His occupation was recorded as a pharmacist, and she is shown as a "pass clerk" with the railroad. This census indicates that he was 30 years of age and was first married at that age. She is listed as age 25, her first marriage occurring at age 20, her marriage to Dewey her second. This census also states that she was born in California and that her father was born in Illinois while her mother was born in Kansas.

The 1940 census has Dewey and Hazel living in Little Rock, Arkansas, and their only son, George Dewey Jr., was 8 years old. They responded in the survey that in 1935 they were living in Memphis. Dewey stated that he was a traveling salesman for a "pharmaceutical house." Hazel did not list any occupation. In response to their level of education, Dewey indicated 4 years of college, Hazel 4 years of high school while George had been in school for 2 years. Dewey reported that he made $4,000 per year.

A 1937 passenger list shows Dewey and Hazel on a cruise from New York City to Hamilton, Bermuda, on July 24, 1937. The list says that they were with the "Squibb Co. Party." They listed their home address as 5216 V. Street, Little Rock, Arkansas. They also were required to list their place of birth. Dewey listed Dickson County, Tennessee, whereas Hazel indicated Red Bluff, California.

108

Red Bluff is about 30 miles south of Redding and 125 miles North of Sacramento.

Although several city directories show the couple living in Little Rock over a long period, a 1955 city directory of Clearwater, Florida, has them living there, where Dewey was listed as a divisional manager for E. R. Squibb & Son.

Their only son, George Jr., was an advertising executive for an ad firm in St. Louis. George Jr. had three children: Bruna Elizabeth, George III and Julie Ann. George III is a successful photographer and has produced movies. He lives in Hollywood, California.

Dewey passed away on September 23, 1989, and Hazel died on May 2, 1974. They are both buried at Memorial Cemetery, Memphis.

These are the 10 children of Henry Clay and Sophronia Matthews Nicks, born over a span of 23 years, between 1876 and 1899. Sophronia was almost 19 years of age when she married, almost 20 years old when she gave birth to her first child and 41 when she had her last child. They lost one child, Bart, when he was 19 years of age.

They were all born into an age of great change and economic evolution. These changes would impact none of them more than Buckner Clay.

Chapter 10
B.C. and Kate, Strength of Character

Buckner Clay Nicks was the third child and first son born to Henry Clay and Sophronia Nicks on August 16, 1881. A second son, Barton, would be born 3 years later in 1884. Barton would never be a healthy child and was never able to provide much help on the farm. The next brother, Emmett, was born in 1889, 8 years later. B. C. would have been 10 years old when Speight was born, 16 years old at Albert's birth and 18 years old when Dewey was born.

His brothers would not have been old enough to provide much of the help needed and expected on the farm during B.C.'s younger years. Certainly, hired help would have been available, but the day-to-day chores expected of a young son would have fallen mostly to B.   As previously mentioned, the U. S. Census of 1890 was destroyed by fire; therefore, we have no written record of B.C. from his birth until the census of 1900, where he is listed in his father's household at the age of 19.

It is safe to assume that he would have spent most of those years working at home and pursuing his education, his world was limited to the Stayton area, where he spent most of his time. The main influences on his formative years would have come through his family and the relationships with his aunts, uncles and grandparents. The formation of his hopes and dreams during his first twenty years would have been influenced by his exposure to those who farmed and engaged in general merchandising.

B. C. Nicks, ca. 1900

Those close relatives that were active in the mercantile business during B.C.'s early years have been covered in a previous chapter. His father was not only a farmer but also owned a large tobacco warehouse. All of these experiences would have made an impression on a young man trying to answer the question of "what will I be when I grow up?"

Mr. Earl Schmittou stated that the earliest school in Stayton was in a log structure located in the same general area as the Friendship Church of Christ. Mrs. Mary Hudgins, who was B.C.'s aunt, taught there in 1895.[65] This is where B.C. would have received his early education.

Later, B.C. would attend the Southside Preparatory School, and Mary Hudgins was teaching there at that time. The 1900 census records Mary as living and teaching in Southside. She is shown in the household of her son, Albert. I have two textbooks that belonged to B.C. One is entitled *School Algebra* and includes a handwritten inscription on the inside: "B. C. Nicks Southside, Tenn., December 2, 1901." The other book is entitled *The Elements of Physics*, and the inscription reads, "B. C. Nicks, Southside Prep. School, Southside, Tenn., Sep 14, 1901." These books place B.C. in Southside, enrolled at the Southside Preparatory School in 1901. He would have been 20 years old.

I have no record of where B.C. was in 1902. He may have been finishing his education, or he may have returned home to farm with his father.

The Marshall & Bruce Company published a directory of Nashville businesses and residents for many years. In the years from 1903 through 1906, B. C. was listed in the Nashville City Directory as living and working in Nashville. In 1903 through 1905 he was residing at the home of his Uncle Anthony Matthews at 1410 Hawkins Avenue, Nashville. This location is between 14th and 16th Avenues South, just about a block west of the present I 440 interstate that transverses Nashville. He is listed as a clerk at the address of 150 2nd Avenue North and Market Street. This may have been the location of Matthew & Phillips Wholesale Grocery in Nashville. It should be noted that 2nd Avenue was once named Market Avenue, and this reference to the location of the Matthew–Phillips wholesale business may have been during this transition.

In 1906 B.C.'s resident address changed to 2904 Poston Ave., Nashville. This was the address of his aunt and uncle, Lena and Robert Nicks. His work address was still listed as 2nd Ave. and Market Street.

B. sent a postcard dated May 2, 1906 to "Miss Kathryn Lyle, Southside Tenn." This card is one that would have been used to inform customers that a salesman would be arriving to make a call. The card states that he would be arriving on "Saturday" and is signed BCN. The company represented is the Herman Bros., Lindauer & Co. of Nashville, a wholesale dry-goods company.

B.C.'s residence may have changed because he changed jobs. There were several wholesale companies located on Market Street. I had always assumed his work place was on the corner of the two streets but now believe that Market Street and 2nd Avenue refer to the same street.

In any case, it would seem that B.C. spent these four years learning the trade of merchandising. The occupation of merchant is one that he would follow for most of his life.

Post Card from B. Nicks to Kate Lyle
May 2, 1906

On April 10, 1907, Buckner Clay Nicks and Martha Katherine Lyle would be married at the home of her parents in Southside. Martha Katherine Lyle (known as Kate) was the eleventh and youngest child born to William James Lyle and Elizabeth Mabry Batson of Southside, Tennessee.

B. would have first become acquainted with Kate through their connections with the Southside Preparatory School. Since he was 4½ years older than Kate, it is not likely they attended classes together. B.C. would have boarded in Southside. The journey from Stayton to Southside would have been a seven or eight mile trip on horseback, much too far to travel on a daily basis.

As noted earlier, B.'s Aunt Mary (Nicks) Hudgins lived in Southside with her son, Albert, and the census states that they boarded students. Kate's oldest sister, Sallie Maria (Lila), was married to the headmaster of the school, Professor William Harper, and they too boarded students. B.C. could have boarded with either of these families.

It is most probable that their courtship occurred after B.C. had left Southside to reside in Nashville. In her diary that documents their first year of marriage, Kate states that they took a walk one afternoon and "burned their letters." These letters are, most likely, correspondence from Nashville to Southside during their courtship.

Much information can be obtained from that diary of their first year together. The following is her first entry that was made on Wednesday, April 10, 1907:

All my brothers and sisters, except A. and Lewis, came this a.m. to see B. and me married. B came about two o'clock and we were quietly married at four by Prof. Harper. We left immediately for Stayton. Were given a supper at B's home where we spent the night. We received a number of beautiful presents. We were both as happy as we could be.

B. C. and Kate Nicks – 1907
Their Wedding Photograph

The next day she wrote that she was not feeling well. They went to his Uncle Frank's (James Franklin Nicks) to spend the next night. The next morning they went to Dull, where they would had their first meal together. There they made their first home with B.C.'s oldest sister, Agnes, and her husband, Elijah Washington Daniel.

Kate's diary offers a very interesting account of 1907. They received many visitors into their home and traveled from time to time to Stayton and to Southside. The distance between Dull and Southside did not seem to limit their mobility; they would travel through Stayton on their way to Southside.

While living here, Kate would give piano lessons at Big Spring Church, which was located almost three miles to the west on the Promise Land Road. She would ride horse back to the church and give lessons all day. B.C. and Kate would attend Church services at either Mt. Hebron Church of Christ or Greenwood Methodist Church. Their mode of transportation was by horseback or buggy.

Kate's family was a large one and Methodist in their faith; she was the youngest of eleven children. A difference of 25 years of age extended between Kate and her oldest sister, Lila. The family was financially very successful in their own right. There has been a book published about her mother's family, which outlines the successes of that family. It is entitled *Southside Cousins,* and the last time I checked, copies could still be purchased.

Without rewriting *Southside Cousins,* I want to list Kate's family and some of the things they accomplished during their lives. Family members are listed in order of birth, and their ages are given as of 1907, the year Kate and B.C. married. This family had a positive impact on the lives of B.C. and Kate and their four sons.

Sallie Maria (Lila) Lyle (11/21/1861–1/17/1946) married William Isham Harper (12/28/1856–12/8/1910). At the time of Kate's marriage, Lila would have been 46 years of age. William Harper was known as Professor Harper, and he performed the marriage ceremony for Kate and B.C. Professor Harper was the head master at Southside Preparatory School, where B.C. got his later education. Both my Father and his brother, Bob, have told me this is where B. and Kate met.

Henry Clay Lyle (8/15/1863–4/11/1943) would have been 44 years old when Kate married. Henry Clay was married to Minnie Lou Harper. They had four children, and their daughter, Mary Elizabeth (Holmes) Lyle (1/12/1891–3/27/1976), was like a sister to Kate. In about 1909 this family moved to Shamrock, Texas.

116

Carney Batson Lyle (7/21/1865–9/3/1938) would have been 41 years old at the time of Kate's marriage. He was married to Minnie Boyd Herndon. Carney Batson Lyle was a prominent attorney in Clarksville.

Annie Lyle (7/11/1867–5/17/1921) would have been 39 years old at the time. She married Edgar Orgain, who founded Orgain Building & Supply Co. in Clarksville. They had a son named William, who married Emma Hudgins, B.C.'s second cousin. Emma Hudgins was the daughter of Albert E. Hudgins and a granddaughter of Mary (Nicks) Hudgins.

Elizabeth "Lizzie" Lyle (10/29/1869–4/18/1923) was the fifth child in Kate's family, and she would have been 37 at the time. I do not know what Lizzie's challenges were, but she was an invalid her entire life. After her parents' deaths in 1910, Lizzie would live with her older sister, Lila, for the remainder of her life.

Matthew G. Lyle (10/10/1872–8/2/1950) would have been 34 at the time. He married Love Rossetter, and they had no children. Matt Lyle was also an attorney. In 1915 he would become the first Attorney General ever elected in Montgomery County, a position he would hold until his death in 1950.

Robert Lyle (5/29/1875–9/26/1876) died at 16 months of age. He was the victim of a tragic accident; he fell into a kettle of scalding water used for sterilizing milking equipment and was so severely burned he never recovered.

John Abram Lyle (3/29/1878–1/2/1947) would have been 29 years old. He was known as A. He married Effie Napier on 4/27/1904. He was living in Birmingham at the time of his death. He was not present at Kate's wedding.

Lewis Lyle (1/4/1880 – 5/20/1971) would have been 27 years old at the time of the wedding. He married Susan Angelina "Angie" Pennington on 1/15/1905. His son, William, became the family "historian" and drew the complete Lyle family tree. In 1918 this marriage produced a son, Robert Eugene, who, at the age of almost 3 years, also fell into a kettle of boiling water in the same house by the same fireplace as did his uncle 45 years earlier. Lewis was not present at the wedding.

James Russell Lyle (8/21/1883 – 2/2/1964) would have been 23 years old when Kate was married and was three years her senior. He was said to have been quite the character.

Another record of these early years is a collection of six letters Kate's mother wrote to Kate dating from May through December in 1909. I have included the full text of these letters in Appendix D. They tell the story of a very difficult time in the lives of Kate's mother and father. They were in declining health and would both pass away in 1910. Her mother obviously missed her youngest daughter and was struggling with what seems to have been the declining mental health of her husband. These letters are also a rare firsthand look at life in the early 20th century. Like Kate's diary of 1907, these letters provide valuable insight into how difficult life was as compared to life as we know it today. This is true particularly for those who were older. There was no social security or long-term care facilities. This could not have been an easy time for Kate.

Kate's father, William James Lyle, would pass away on February 5, 1910, and her mother, Elizabeth Mabry Batson Lyle, would die on April 26, 1910. They are buried at Greenwood Cemetery in Clarksville, Tennessee.

While this book is essentially about the family of B.C. Nicks, it is important to note that the influence of Kate's family

118

made as large an impact on her children as did the Nicks family.

B.C.'s and Kate's first two children would be born in Dull. James Henry Nicks was born on April 9, 1909, and Robert Lyle Nicks was born on October 21, 1911. When James was born, Kate's mother wrote in one of her letters a warning about the dangers of catching the croup and advised her to keep "little James" away from "those Daniel children."

As has been discussed previously, the general merchandise store was a central part of life in small communities during B.C.'s formative years. Both his mother's and father's families had been extensively involved in the trade that was a central part of every community.

Daniel & Nicks Mercantile Wagon
Seated in the wagon – E. W. Daniel
L-R Agnes Daniel, son William in her arms, Kate Nicks

B.C. and Kate began their married life as partners in a general merchandising store with his sister, Agnes, and her husband, E. W. Daniel. The name of the business was Daniel, Nicks & Company, and their store was located in Dull. The community of Dull is located on Highway 49, about halfway between Charlotte and Ashland City, Tennessee.

119

The store was situated on property that had been previously owned by the Doty family. The store utilized a covered mercantile wagon to travel the area buying eggs, meat and produce from local families that would in turn be sold at the store.

This venture was probably a challenge from the beginning because the Daniel-Nicks store was in direct competition with one of the largest general stores in the area, the Ben Sensing General Store. This store was comparable in size to the Speight/Nicks store in Stayton and was located only about 500 feet down the road from the Daniel Nicks store. The competition would have been tough.

Sometime before 1910, E. W. Daniel would leave the partnership and move his family to Dickson. The 1910 census lists Mr. Daniel as living in Dickson. There he would become the manager of Dickson Wholesale Grocery. Dickson Wholesale Grocery was a stock company (corporation) that was owned by various shareholders in the Dickson community. Mr. Daniel made his first home in Dickson on Walnut Street and then later on Center Avenue.

B.C. was now the sole proprietor of the store in Dull, and deed records show that he purchased the property where the store was located from Nick Loggins. That purchase was made on September 30, 1908, which would have made his partnership with Mr. Daniel a short one. Kate's diary relates that B.C.'s brother, Emmett, came and visited them on occasion, and he most certainly would have been expected to assist at the store. Emmett would have been 18 years old at the time, and the brothers would later become partners in several business ventures.

At some point this store was closed, and the family thereafter embarked on a new and larger general merchandise store in the White Oak Flat, only 1.5 miles down Highway 49, named Nicks Brothers. The exact timing of this move is not known; however, we know that their second son, Robert Lyle, was born in Dull in October 21, 1911. Deed records show us that the store property in Dull was sold on December 6, 1911. The purchaser was Ben Sensing, who owned the large store up the road. B.C. had purchased the property in 1908 for $125, selling it in 1911 for the same amount.

The price structure of land, as well as all goods and services, was much different from what we are accustomed to today. The value of a dollar was much higher, and they did not live under the tax system that we do today. In order to place this in perspective, we should remember that in 1927, Henry and Sophronia Nicks required only $100 per year to maintain their lifestyle, according to the agreement with their son, Emmett.

In 1915, B.C. and Kate's third son, Carney, my father, was born in White Oak Flat. The move to White Oak Flat had occurred sometime between the birth of their second son, Bob in 1911, and Carney in 1915.

At White Oak Flat, B.C. and his brother Emmett would begin a new general merchandising store named Nicks Brothers. This would be a much larger store than the Daniel-Nicks establishment with all the goods and services that were made available by the Sensing store and the Speight/Nicks store. In 1914 Emmett married Mary Larkins in her father's house on Jones Creek Road. It was a small gathering; the only family of Emmett's that attended were B.C. and Kate.

In 2010 I was fortunate to have had the opportunity to meet and talk to Frankie Caldwell, who lived her entire life in the Dull/White Oak Flat community. At the time she was approaching her 100th birthday. Her father had worked for "Mr. B." hauling groceries and other goods from Dickson to the Nicks Brothers store. She told me that she distinctly remembered Mr. B. and Miss Kate going down the road in their horse and buggy. Miss Frankie said, "I have never seen a more handsome couple anywhere."

Nicks Brothers Script

Miss Frankie gave me a piece of Nicks Brothers script that was used by the store to pay individuals for goods and labor. This script was in coin fashion, made of copper and about the diameter of our half dollar, but much thinner. The script could only be spent on items that were purchased at the store, and her father had been paid in this fashion. One side is imprinted with "$10.00, Nicks Bros.," the other side with "$10.00, In Trade Only. Pat 1914." The use of script was common in those days in the larger stores and serves as another example of the scarcity of money and credit at that time. The general store was truly the grocery, farm implement dealer, post office and bank to the community that it served.

Besides being a merchant, B.C. also bought and sold other properties during this period, according to Dickson County deeds. Between 1909 and 1920, deed records show that B.C. bought six different pieces of property in the Dull/White Oak Flat area. These properties ranged in size and price from 2.5 acres costing $60 to 120 acres at a cost of $781. These are the total purchase prices, not the price per acre.

Deed records also show that in about 1915 he would become a partner in a general store in White Bluff with Mr. J. W.

Brown. Presently, I am researching this purchase and hope to talk with some of Mr. Brown's descendants, but so far I have had no success in my search for the details. I never heard about this store from my Dad or his brothers, but I did know that B.C. was close to many of the families in White Bluff.

In 1917 B.C. and Emmett were required to register for the draft due to our Country's involvement in World War I. Emmett's registration is dated June 5, 1917, and states that he was a merchant. B.C.'s registration is dated September 12, 1918, and states that he was also merchant. They both state that they work with the Nicks Brothers Company. Based upon these registration documents, we can conclude that Nicks Brothers Company was still in operation in September of 1918.

The process of change is continuous and endlessly complex. By the end of the decade, many changes were underway in rural America that would have a huge impact on B.C., Kate and their family. The world in which B.C. had grown up was one where communities were separated from one another because of limited means of transportation and, therefore, communication. Telephones were scarce and radios were nonexistent. Frederick Lewis Allen states in his book, *The Big Change, America Transforms Itself, 1900–1950* that "each town and each farm was far more dependent upon its own resources, produce and social contacts in 1895 than in 1918. Their horizons were close to them. They lived among familiar people and familiar things—individuals and families of their own sort. A man's success or failure seemed more likely than in later years to depend upon forces and events within his own range of vision."[66]

It was in this world that the general merchandising store had become the center of each community and would make its owner a necessity of everyday life. The merchant stood at the center of the rural economy. There were three main reasons for this dependency.

First, there was no credit available to speak of, and the farmer was dependent upon the merchant to provide him the goods and services necessary to provide for his family. Failure to pay at the end of each year could lead to foreclosure if the credit was secured by the farm. This often led to merchants being known as the "landlords of the community."

Second, there was no rural free mail delivery. The general store most often served as the post office. Mail would arrive at the nearest train station and be delivered by a private carrier to the general store for pickup by the customer. When Sears & Roebuck first began to mail catalogs to local residents, they would have been delivered to the general store for pickup by the recipient. It was common practice among merchants to destroy all but one of these free catalogs, which the store would then make available to its customers if they desired to make an order. If one was able to gain access to a catalog independent of the store, the order would have been delivered to the store for pickup by the customer. Not a good thing if the customer owed the general store for a year's worth of subsistence.

Finally, the lack of transportation made for dependence on the local community. A trip from White Oak Flat to Dickson required a journey of about 14 miles. This would have taken most of a day, one way, requiring an overnight stay to rest the horse. Most of the small communities and general stores of the day existed to bring commodities together in a central location for resale to the consumer.

By 1918 changes had begun that would eventually lead to the disappearance of the general store as the center of community life. These changes did not happen overnight but were gradually implemented, changing the life of the merchant forever.

Consider this. In 1895 there were 300 cars in the United States. By 1905 the number had risen to 78,000, and by 1914 there was an estimated 1.7 million cars on the road in the United States.[67]

Not only did this increase the mobility of the public but also provided for an increase in the availability of jobs that were not on the farm. The family no longer had to harness a horse to a wagon for a trip to the general store but could now get into their automobile and drive 10 miles to save 25 cents on a loaf of bread that was on sale at a larger establishment.

In terms of credit, banks began to appear in small communities everywhere and were more than ready to extend credit not only for farm production but also for consumer goods. Currency had suddenly become a necessity and was readily available to those who were moving to larger towns for jobs that were better than those available on the farm.

Rural Free Delivery (RFD) began late in the 19th century. Initially, the proposal to offer free mail delivery to the home was not universally embraced, as private carriers and local merchants feared a loss of business. The practice became mandatory in 1896, but the process of implementation was a massive undertaking, and most areas were not served with delivery to a roadside mailbox until about 1910.[68] The availability of mail delivery to the home not only allowed for the delivery of the mail order catalog, but also insured that the package would be delivered to the home, which would completely bypass the local merchant. No matter the contents of the package, each box carried more than an inert product; it brought an implicit message: this is the new way of the new world.

On March 6, 1918, B.C. and Kate's youngest son, Lyle Matthews Nicks, was born, completing their family of four boys. James would have been almost 9 years of age; Bob would have been 6½ and Carney almost 3 years old. The family would have still been living in White Oak Flat.

On October 25, 1919, B.C. and Emmett and their wives entered into a transaction that would have a tremendous impact on their futures. They purchased a 320-acre farm in Rutherford

County, outside the city of Murfreesboro, on the Manchester Highway, for a sum of $25,600. The sellers were J. C. Couch and his wife Lula Mai. This would have been a large sum for the times and was particularly so when considering the price of other lands B.C. had bought over the previous 10 years.

The deed states that the property was on the west side of the Murfreesboro to Manchester Road. The area is developed today, and it appears that Interstate 24 now crosses the property. To date, I have not been able to identify the specific property, but all of the land in that area would have been prime farmland in 1919.

The terms of the transaction state that $5,100 was paid in cash. The balance of the purchase price was in the form of two notes, one in the amount of $4,000 due on January 1, 1921, and the other in the amount $3,331.26 due January 1, 1926. The remainder of the purchase price would be paid by B.C. and Emmett assuming the balance of five additional notes that Mr. Couch owed to M. T. Holman and Mrs. Annie P. Holman. These notes were for $467.78 due January 1, 1921, $2,977.78 due January 1, 1922, $2,977.78 due January 1, 1923 and two other notes of $3,000 each due on January 1, 1924 and 1925 respectively. All of the notes were secured by a lien on the property in favor of Couch and Holman. Possession of the property was to be given on January 1, 1920.

The census of the 15th Civil District of Dickson County was taken on January 8, 1920, and shows us that changes had been made in the family. All four of B.'s sons were living at home. In this census, B.C. lists his occupation as "farmer." B.C. and Kate did not own but rented the home they were living in. They lived on the Charlotte Road, which in White Oak Flat is known as Highway 49.

Looking "up and down" the road in the 1920 census, one notes who their neighbors were. Four doors down lived Emmett and Mary with their two daughters—Sarah Louise, 4 years old, and

126

Claytie Lee, 2 weeks old. Emmett was also renting a house and his occupation is listed as a farmer.

Seven doors down the road in the same direction lived Marvin Duke and his family, including a son named Wagner, who was 3½ years old. My Dad (Carney Nicks) told me that the first person he could remember knowing at the White Oak School was Wagner Duke.

Two doors down in the opposite direction lived Allen Doty and his wife, Dora. Allen is listed as 37 years old, one year younger than B.C., and the census shows his occupation as an owner/operator of a general mercantile store. The Doty's were good friends of B.C. and Kate, and Mrs. Doty would later board with Kate in Dickson for several years after B.C. passed away.

I cannot pinpoint the exact time, but it appears that B.C. and Emmett left the mercantile business between mid-1918 and mid-1919. I have found no real estate records at this time that would indicate a sale of any type. Looking through the 1920 census records, I have found no other persons, other than the Doty family, who listed themselves as merchants. Today there is no building standing where the Nicks Brothers Store was located; there is only a vacant lot. Some of the older residents who presently live in the area have told me that they remember a store being located there as late as 1945, but no one remembers who owned it.

Whatever the case, it appears that the brothers were no longer involved with the general store and that they were, at that time, farmers. Whatever the reason for the change, it happened quickly. We know that in September of 1918 in his draft registration, B.C. listed his occupation as a merchant with Nicks Brothers and fifteen months later the brothers had purchased a large farm in Rutherford County and were farming for a living.

The purchase of this farm would not have a good outcome and would have lasting effects on both families. There is little documentation of their specific movements over the next 6 years, but we can infer some of the information known from family sources to track their movements.

While I do not know when, I believe that Emmett moved his family to Murfreesboro to run the farm. Nancy Nicks Norton has told me that her father, James, had told her about going to Murfreesboro to work on the farm. Both Bob and Carney Nicks told me how hard it was to work for Emmett, but until I found out about the Rutherford County farm, I had always assumed they were talking about working in Stayton. Considering the ages of Carney and Bob, they would not have been old enough to work for Emmett at Stayton prior to the Murfreesboro purchase.

The farm investment did not work out. As agricultural prices fell and the notes began to mature, B.C. and Emmett could not pay them or the interest that was due. The story that I have been told was they traded their way out of the farm for a "store of goods" that they later moved to Dickson.

On December 24, 1924, B.C. and Kate would sell their undivided one half-interest in the store building and lot they owned in White Bluff to their partner, J. W. Brown. The selling price was $2,250.00. Mr. Brown and B.C. had been partners for several years, and one must assume, given the timing of this sale, that B.C. was disposing of assets in order to pay notes that were maturing.

On January 5, 1926, B.C. and Kate would sell the last tract of land that they owned at the time, 61 acres located in the Dull community, for a price of $1,500. Again, the timing of the sale corresponds with the due dates of notes that were given for the purchase of the Rutherford County farm.

Finally, on August 7, 1926, B.C. and Emmett sold the 320 acres in Rutherford County to J. W. Odom and his wife, May L. Odom. The purchase price was $17,800, a loss of $7,800 based on the purchase price of $25,600. This would not have included any interest payments or operating losses that may have occurred. Six years and 10 months had passed since they had purchased the property.

There is no mention in the deed of any trade for a store of goods, although that does not preclude the possibility. The deed states that the consideration for the purchase was made with $8,000 in cash and the assumption of a note owed to the Federal Farm Loan Bank of Louisville, Kentucky, for $9,800. The deed states that this note was taken out by B.C. and Emmett on November 7, 1925. It further states that this sale was made according to the plan promulgated by the Federal Farm Loan Bank. In my view, this last language simply means that the loan was called and a workout solution was approved and most likely proposed by the Bank.

Because we think that a store of goods was received and brought to Dickson, it is probable that some of the cash consideration was in store goods.

While many mark the beginning of the depression with the crash of the stock market in 1929, the crash in agriculture prices occurred in 1920. The emergence of the United States as an economic power in the early 1900s fostered a worldwide boom in agriculture products. This boom accelerated as World War I disrupted European agriculture; however, the European countries recovered quickly, and production resumed faster than expected after the war's sudden end. As a result, agricultural prices plummeted in 1920 and declined through much of the decade. The price of a bushel of wheat fell from $3.08 in May 1920 to $1.68 in December of the same year. The price of a bushel of corn fell from $2.00 to $0.76 over the same period.[69] For B. C. and Emmett the depression had begun. B.C. would not live to see the recovery.

Further evidence that Emmett resided in Murfreesboro during these years is provided in this deed. When they sold the farm, signatures on the deed had to be notarized. B.C. and Kate's signatures were notarized by Joe Crosby at the First National Bank

129

in Dickson. Emmett and Mary's signatures were notarized by E. C. Holloway in Rutherford County, Tennessee.

Again, the Rutherford County deed was dated in August of 1926. In March of 1927, B.C. and Emmett's father, Henry Clay, would enter into a contract with Emmett that would insure Henry and Sophronia's long-term care. In that contract, Henry states that Emmett was now living in the house of his parents and cultivating their farm. By April of 1928, both Henry and Sophronia had passed away, and in December of 1928 the children would agree to sell the farm to Emmett for $6,000. This farm consisted of almost 300 acres, which provides a good idea of how expensive the Rutherford County farm really was.

Emmett would remain on the home place and farm it until March of 1948, when he would sell it to W. L. Jackson and Ewing Jackson for the sum of $15,000.

On February 5, 2000, Clay Nicks, son of Albert Nicks, appeared on a local radio show that interviewed local residents of Dickson regarding the history of Dickson and Dickson County. Warren Medley, host of the show, asked Clay about the beginnings of Nicks Hardware Store.

Clay responded that through a real estate deal in the late 1920s, Albert's brothers (B.C. and Emmett) came into possession of a store of goods located on South Main Street in Dickson next to the "old Springer Store." Albert was farming on Jones Creek Road with his father-in-law at the time. Clay further stated that Emmett was busy farming the "home place" and that B.C. was an outside sales representative for the Dickson Wholesale Grocery Company, meaning that neither had the time to run a store. B.C. and Emmett brought in Albert to run the store.

Clay also stated that there was too much competition on South Main Street for an additional grocery store to be successful. There were two others, the Springer Market and Walker's Grocery. Through his connections as a sales representative for the Dickson

Wholesale Grocery, B.C. knew of a vacant store building in Wrigley, Tennessee, and the inventory was moved there, reinventing the Nicks Brothers Company.

The 1930 census shows Albert Nicks living on Murrell Street in Dickson. His occupation is listed as a merchant, and the census states that he was the manager of a grocery store. Sometime soon after 1930, Albert would move his family to Wrigley where they would stay for about 10 years. Their son, Clay, attended his first year of high school in Centerville.

It appears that B.C. and Kate moved to Dickson in the fall of 1921. Nancy Nicks Norton, daughter of James, provided me with her father's first reports cards from Dickson. These report cards show that B.C. and Kate moved to Dickson in the fall of 1921. There were five grading periods in each semester during that time, and James entered the 6th grade in Dickson during the third grading period of the first semester. These cards also show that James attended the 7th grade in Dickson and was promoted from the 7th grade to Dickson High School, where he would graduate in 1926 at the age of 17.

My Dad always said that he attended the first grade at the White Oak Flat School, but he was never able to locate that report card. Based on the time line established by James's cards, Dad would have started the first grade in White Oak Flat but later transferred mid-semester to Dickson when the family moved. This might explain the missing card.

In a radio interview on the Old Timers Program in 2001, Bob Nicks stated that when his parents moved to Dickson, they first lived on North Main Street. Later, B.C. and Kate would move their family to McCreary Heights, where they would rent a house from Rafe Nicks, who was the father of Carl Nicks. This house would later become the home of Carl and Ida Nicks

In a news story published in the Nashville *Tennessean* that reported on B. C.'s death, it was stated that he moved to Dickson

131

in 1926 to become associated with Dickson Wholesale Grocery Company.[70] However, an article from the *Tennessean* in 1923 that was reporting on business conditions in Dickson spoke of several Dickson salesmen who were optimistic over conditions leading up to the Christmas season. One of the salesmen mentioned in the 1923 article was B. C. Nicks.[71]

These two pieces of information seem to be in conflict with each other with respect to when B.C. and Kate moved to Dickson. Perhaps B.C. was a salesman in Dickson but still residing in White Oak Flat. This, however, seems doubtful, considering the distance he would have had to travel and considering the evidence provided by James's report cards.

The news article written about his passing could be in error, and there is no way of knowing who was the source of this information, most likely not Kate. This article also states that they moved so that B.C. could be associated with Dickson Wholesale Company, for which the 1923 article states he was a salesman.

Home of B. C. and Kate Nicks
304 East College Street, Dickson, Tennessee

B.C. and Kate purchased their first home in Dickson on May 5, 1927. The home was located on the corner of Herman

Avenue and East College Street. It was purchased for $2,500 from the Fourth & First National Bank of Nashville, which had recently foreclosed on the property. This would be the home that all of their grandchildren would remember.

As stated earlier, B.C. and E. W. Daniel were partners in a small mercantile store in Dull named Daniel & Nicks Company. Mr. Daniel would leave this partnership in about 1909 and move to Dickson to manage Dickson Wholesale Grocery.

The purpose of a wholesale grocery business in 1910 was to move goods down the supply line to the local merchant. Because of the limited avenues of transportation available, the largest of these concerns would be located in the larger cities, with smaller wholesale businesses located in outlying towns where distribution would then be made to the general merchandising stores that were located throughout the county.

An example of this would be the Matthews & Phillips Wholesale Company in Nashville, selling to Dickson Wholesale Grocery in Dickson, which would sell to Nicks Brothers General Store in White Oak Flat. Salesmen would be employed at the wholesale companies to call upon local stores in a given area. In this instance, Anthony Matthews (B.C.'s uncle) was a partner in the Matthews & Phillips Wholesale Grocery and B.C.'s brother-in-law, E. W. Daniel, was the manager of the Dickson Wholesale Grocery. B.C. was employed as a salesman for Dickson Wholesale Grocery.

Dickson Wholesale Grocery was a stock company (today we would refer to it as a corporation) that was owned by various shareholders, some of whom were individuals that lived and worked in the community and some businesses that felt the investment necessary to the growth of the community. Credit needed for the operation was made available through this system. Matthews & Phillips would sell on credit to Dickson Wholesale, which in turn would sell on credit to the general merchandise stores. This unwieldy arrangement was made necessary by the lack of sufficient credit. This method of doing business would change rapidly during the first 30 years of the 1900s.

By 1920, B.C. no longer listed himself as a merchant, but as a farmer. By 1923 he was employed as a salesman with Dickson Wholesale Grocery, which was being run by his brother-in-law, E. W. Daniel. The changes in credit and retail sales probably created a situation with Nicks Brothers that prohibited it from being profitable enough to raise a family that included four boys.

In 1922, the year after B.C. moved his family to Dickson, Dickson Wholesale Grocery would purchase a building where they would relocate the business. I do not know where they were located prior to 1922. On May 18, 1922, Dickson Wholesale Grocery would purchase a two-story building from a Mr. W. A. Chambers of Clarksville for $8,500. This building was located in Dickson on the southwest corner of Main and Railroad Streets. The structure would later be occupied by Nicks Hardware until 2015, when it was demolished.

In December of 1927, 7 months after B.C. bought his first home, the shareholders of Dickson Wholesale Grocery met and voted to amend their charter to increase their capital account from $35,330 to $50,000.[72] Increasing cash through the issue of new capital would mean either that the business was growing fast and that individuals wanted to buy stock, or that the business was running short of cash and needed to raise capital.

The amendment lists the directors of the corporation at that time as S. G. Robinson (president of First National Bank), J. E. Crosby (cashier of First National Bank), G. W. Pursley (secretary of Dickson Wholesale Grocery), B. C. Nicks and E. W. Daniel.

On November 2, 1929, Dickson Wholesale Grocery sold their building to Mr. Dan E. Beasley. The purchase price was $10,000—$4,500 paid in cash and the balance paid by the assumption of a note of $5,500 that Dickson Wholesale Co. owed to First Trust & Security Bank of Dickson. First Trust & Security Bank was a subsidiary of First National Bank in Dickson and was wholly owned by First National Bank.

There are some interesting aspects to these transactions. First, when Dickson Wholesale Company filed to amend their charter in 1927, two of the five directors were senior officers of First National Bank. Secondly, D. E. Beasley, the purchaser of the building, was the mayor of Dickson and one of First National Bank's larger shareholders. (His grandson, Dan Beasley Andrews would become President of First National in the late 1960s, succeeding S. G. Robinson.) Keep in mind that E. W. Daniel was also a director at First National at that time.

It would appear that Dickson Wholesale Grocery had fallen on hard times and that the raising of capital and the sale of the building were attempts to save the business and to work out of debt. Further language in the deed lends itself to this thinking. Robert Orr & Company, a large wholesale grocer in Nashville, had to agree to the sale in writing, which means that Dickson Wholesale was indebted to Robert Orr & Company.

The sale took place on November 2, 1929. The 1930 census was taken in April of 1930. E. W. Daniel listed himself as being retired; he was 61 years of age and living on Center Avenue in Dickson. He would pass away on October 15, 1934, from a stroke that resulted in paralysis caused by hypertension. The attending physician was Dr. R. P. Beasley.

In December of 1934 a deed passed ownership to all of the remaining property, both real and personal, owned by Dickson Wholesale Grocery Company to Agnes Nicks Daniel, E.W.'s widow. The deed states that Mrs. Daniel had become the owner of all the shares of stock in Dickson Wholesale Grocery Company and that the company's charter was surrendered on January 4, 1930. It further states that E. W. Daniel had been appointed as trustee of the remaining assets, that final disposition of the assets

135

had been underway for several years and that upon Mr. Daniel's death, B. C. Nicks had been appointed substitute-liquidating trustee. Since Mrs. Daniel had acquired all of the outstanding shares of the company, B. C. Nicks transferred these assets to Mrs. Daniel.

The assets listed in the disposition include the following matters of interest. Included were 60 acres of land located on Piney Creek in Dickson County, 10 shares of stock in the Dickson Development Company, 2 shares of stock in the Dickson County Cooperative Sweet Potato Association and 6 shares of stock in the Dickson County Cooperative Creamery Association. Also included were various other notes, accounts and personal property.

Obviously, the late 1920s would have been a tough time for the B. C. Nicks family, as well as for the families of his sister, Agnes, and his brother, Emmett. It should be understood that the economic challenges and disappointments that occurred during the 1920s should not be viewed as failures but rather as huge economic challenges that produced hard times for the family. I have heard my Dad say many times, "If we had been the only family to have been experiencing hard times during the Depression, I'm sure I would have felt bad about our circumstances, but I didn't because everyone was in the same boat."

The great depression was a collapse of terrifying proportions and duration. We date the Panic of 1929 as the beginning, but the duration would last until the early 1940s, when wartime production would provide the boost needed to expand jobs and wages. Nevertheless, the Depression marked millions of people inwardly for the rest of their lives.

During B.C.'s lifetime, the world had changed from one where success was determined by events within one's own range of vision, to one where life's events were dictated by national and global events far beyond any individual's control or even

136

knowledge. It was as if some invisible force had changed the rules without telling anyone.

Many individuals and families, who had worked hard and laid out plans to provide for their families were devastated by the events of the 1920s. The damage seemed to begin in the smallest of communities immediately after World War I and then rolled down the street right on to the next level and then the next. Today, our impressions of the Depression years are formed by images of men standing in long lines for a job or a handout, families with all of their possessions loaded in a truck leaving town on a dusty road or simply a picture of a malnourished family on the front porch of an old dilapidated cabin. While it is true that these images did portray the plight of some, not everyone was affected in this manner, but be sure that everyone was affected. The life of B. C. Nicks cannot be measured by the economic misfortunes that beset him in the 1920s, but rather by the manner in which he responded to those events in the 1930s.

The 1930 census was taken in April and shows B.C. and Kate living on East College Street. All four of the boys are listed as living at home, none indicated as employed. Even though Dickson Wholesale Grocery Company had surrendered its charter on January 4, 1930, after selling the building in December of 1929, B.C. listed his employment as the manager of a dry-goods store.

The impact that the beginnings of the Depression had on our family is illustrated in their movements between 1920 and 1930. In 1920, B.C. was living in White Oak Flat and was farming. Emmett moved to Murfreesboro to run the newly purchased farm there, and Albert was home farming with his father. Two years later, Albert married and began farming with his father-in-law, Sam Fussell.

The two events that triggered the rapid movement of these three brothers were the failure of the farming endeavor in Murfreesboro and the closing of Dickson Wholesale Grocery.

137

After the farm dispersal, Emmett moved back home with his parents and Albert moved to Dickson to work in the new Nicks Brothers Store stocked by dry goods received from the sale of the farm. When Dickson Wholesale failed, B. was forced to employ himself in the new Dickson store where he worked with Albert. While the store may not have produced enough profits for both families to live on, it did provide groceries that would feed the families.

In 2015, at the Nicks Hardware dispersal sale, I acquired several ledger books of the Nicks Brothers store that recorded items that were purchased on account by various customers during the 1930s. Among these ledger books were those used by B.C. and Albert to account for items they personally took from the store. They each charged their purchases on account and would "settle up" with each other at year's end. According to these ledgers, this arrangement was still in place as late as 1936. Prices for various goods that reflect values at that time are included in Appendix E.

It would become apparent that two families could not survive on the proceeds of the store. In fact, competition on South Main Street would not allow for the support of even one family. The decision was made to move the store along with Albert's family to Wrigley, Tennessee, where he would take sole responsibility for its management.

During the summer of 1930, B.C. would make the decision to enter county politics and run for the Office of Trustee. The Office of Trustee is responsible for the collection of property taxes, for the disbursement of funds and for serving generally as the financial officer for the county. The trustee is also responsible for making periodic financial reports to the County Commission (known as the Quarterly Court during this period).

Election to the Office of Trustee would have been vital for B.C. in terms of being able to remain in Dickson and to provide for his family. B.C. would have been 49 years old at the time and

138

without a paycheck. Kate was 44 years of age, and James, Bob, Carney and Lyle were 21, 19, 16 and 13, respectively. James would have been preparing to graduate from Pharmacy School in Memphis. Bob was preparing to enter U.T. Knoxville in the fall. Carney and Lyle were attending school in Dickson. Kate would have a hysterectomy in the fall. Overall, the pressure must have been enormous.

Slayden Hunt was the incumbent trustee and had held the office for about 10 years. The trustee was then elected for a two-year term. Mr. Hunt was the father of Miss Kathleen Hunt, who would marry Dorris Harris on August 14, 1940. Dorris Harris's father was Melvin Harris, who was the County Court clerk and was also seeking reelection. Mr. Hunt and Mr. Harris were close associates and friends.

Geographically, B.C. would have had an advantage over Mr. Hunt in a two-man race. While Mr. Hunt had lived in Dickson longer than B.C. and was from the Yellow Creek Community, B.C. was well known in the northern parts of the county and had been an active merchant in the White Bluff area. B.C. had also traveled the county for at least 7 years representing the Dickson Wholesale Grocery.

However, an easy race it was not to be. Recognizing that a two-man race would be a tough proposition, Mr. Hunt's supporters talked Slayden Phillips into entering the race. Slayden Phillips was a lifelong resident of the Stayton community, operated a general store there and, worst of all, he was B.'s first cousin. Slayden Phillips's mother was Jane Phillips, a sister to B.C.'s mother, Sophronia.

The county was then divided into 15 voting districts with 20 voting precincts throughout the county. B.C. Nicks carried 10 boxes and Slayden Hunt carried 10. Slayden Phillips did not carry a box and would finish second in only three boxes. B.C. would total 1,708 votes and win the race by 112 votes out of 3,936 votes

139

cast. Mr. Hunt's strategy of splitting up the vote almost worked. In fact, it would have worked if not for B.C.'s large margin of 121 combined votes in White Bluff and Claylick. (See Appendix F.)

I recall my Dad talking about the importance of B.C. being elected and what that job would mean to the family. It was a steady income and his only other source of income at that time would have been working in the Nicks Brothers store with Albert.

On September 5, 1930, B.C. was sworn in as the new trustee of Dickson County, as was the new County Court clerk, Lee Mathis, who had defeated Mr. Melvin Harris. Mr. Harris did not want to surrender his office and asked for a recount, which appears to have been declined. Mr. Hunt did step aside and concede his office to B.C. but requested that he be allowed to give his final quarterly report to the County Court.

The request was granted and on October 6, 1930, Mr. Hunt appeared before the court and gave his final financial report. The county Judge was Joe B. Weems (the father of Jimmy Weems, who would also serve as county judge some 20 years later). At the conclusion of his report, Mr. Hunt requested that Judge Weems have an audit conducted of the Trustee's Office for the last year that he had served. The County Court did more than concur with the request; they authorized Judge Weems to have a certified auditor review the books of the office for the entire 10 years that Mr. Hunt had held office.

Mr. Hunt had leased a service station in November of 1930 located on the southwest corner of College Street and Church Street in Dickson. His future son-in-law, Dorris Harris, ran the station. The audit results were soon released and discrepancies were found in the books. On January 18, 1931, Mr. Hunt would take his own life in the restroom of that service station.

Some of the information regarding B.'s election to the Office of Trustee was taken from back issues of the *Dickson Herald* that are available at the Dickson County Library. In researching

140

this election, I also found other items regarding our family's activities during this period.

The September 12, 1930, issue of the *Dickson Herald* reported that Dr. W. C. Jackson (no relation to the Jackson brothers who later moved to Dickson and established Goodlark Hospital) had purchased the Jackson-Duke Drug store from his partner. This article further stated that James Nicks, who had graduated from Pharmacy School at the University of Tennessee in Memphis the previous spring, was assisting Dr. Jackson at the store.

In November of 1930 the *Dickson Herald* reported that on Sunday evening, November 2, the residence of B.C. Nicks was burglarized between the hours of 6 P.M. and 10 P.M. Two watches, a traveling bag, a suit and other items of wearing apparel were taken. The items of clothing were reported to have belonged to James and Carney. B.C. and Kate were reported to have been in White Bluff for the evening visiting friends and, on returning home, found the house generally ransacked. There were no clues as to the identity of the burglars.[73]

In December of 1930 the *Dickson Herald* reported that Bob Nicks was home from the University of Tennessee in Knoxville. Another article that month stated that B. C. Nicks had been elected as a director of the Chamber of Commerce.

In 1932 B.C. would run for reelection for the Office of Trustee. This time he would be unopposed and would receive 2,737 votes.

In 1934, B.C. would run for his third and final term as Trustee; however, this was another close election. He would face opposition from two other candidates, Melvin Holland and J. H. Cunningham. Mr. Holland was from Dickson while Mr. Cunningham resided on the north side of the county. B.C. would again prevail with 1,565 votes to 1,374 votes for Mr. Holland and

141

1,149 votes for Mr. Cunningham. B.C.'s margin of victory was only 191 votes.

My Dad told me that these elections were very hard affairs, creating much stress and fatigue over the summer months, as B. would travel the county meeting the public and soliciting votes. He would not seek reelection in 1936.

News articles in the *Dickson Herald* during the mid-1930s show that B.C. was very involved in the community. He was active in the Chamber of Commerce, serving as chairman of the Membership Committee, first vice president and later as president of the Chamber.

B.C. was also involved with the Fair Board, serving one year as chairman of the Livestock Committee and another year heading up the Premiums Committee. Kate was also a member of the MacDowell Music Club and served as their president in 1936. They were both members of the Walnut Street Church of Christ. B.C.'s obituary would state that he was an elder there. (I have always understood that he was a deacon, not an elder).

The following is a note that Kate wrote to B.C. on Father's Day, June 16, 1935.

My dearest Sweetheart:-

How happy we are—this day set apart for the Fathers of our country. We know we have the best Father of all. We appreciate your Christian Character above everything—and you have been good and kind to us always.

We hope and pray you may be spared to us many more years and that your years to come will be filled with happiness and comfort.

One who loves you most devotedly -
Kate

The 1930s saw their children grow and prosper. James was a Pharmacist and by 1935, along with J. W. Beasley, had purchased the Jackson Drug Store. Bob would become the owner of City Service Dry Cleaners in 1932, and Carney would graduate from High School as the president of his class in 1933. In 1935 Carney would teach school at Oakmont Elementary, after spending two years at David Lipscomb College. Lyle would graduate from high school as the salutatorian of his class and enroll in Pepperdine College in Los Angles, California.

Another Depression era event that would affect B.C. was the closing of the Banks in 1933, known as the Bank Holiday. On Saturday, March 4, 1933, the day of his inauguration, President Roosevelt announced that beginning on Monday, March 6, 1933 all banks would be closed.[74] By March 15, all banks that were allowed to reopen had done so. Over 4,000 banks in the U.S. would remain closed.[75]

In Dickson, there were two banks, First National Bank and Citizens National Bank. Only First National was allowed to reopen, meaning that the depositors at Citizens National Bank had been placed under receivership and that customer deposits were at risk. There was no such thing as deposit insurance at that time.

The depositors of Citizens National Bank held a meeting at the Bank. (It was located at the present location of the Bank of Dickson's Main Street office.) The group selected Mr. E. W. Stewart to be spokesman for the group and selected B. C. Nicks to act as Secretary. (I have seen a copy of those minutes but am unable to locate them.)

The group agreed that they would offer to sell their deposits to First National at 50 cents on the dollar in an effort to "merge" their interests. There was not another bank located in Dickson at the time, and First National rejected the idea. There would not be another bank in Dickson until 1954, when the Bank of Dickson was granted a charter by the State of Tennessee.

One cannot blame First National Bank for not agreeing to purchase the deposits of Citizens National Bank's customers. The depositors had nothing to sell because the Bank was under the control of the federal government. Citizens National had been placed under the receivership of the Federal Reserve, which would be responsible for collecting assets and distributing any deposits that remained to the customer. The State of Tennessee was also a depositor at Citizens National, and records show that they had not received any monies on their deposits as late as 1940. On December 14, 1933, the directors of First National Bank passed a resolution making the necessary arrangements to become a depository for the receiver of the Citizens National Bank.[76]

What should be called into question however is the manner in which some banks were allowed to reopen while some would remain closed.

The decision to declare a "bank holiday" was announced by newly elected President Franklin Roosevelt, on a Sunday, less than 24 hours after his inauguration. All banks remained closed the following week while the Federal Reserve Banks and National Bank Examiners determined which banks were sound enough to reopen. Only one week was given to decide matters of extreme importance.

I have been told by several older people that the two banks that were in Dickson were of equal strength. One was no stronger than the other. However, one was more politically connected than the other was.

Senator Kenneth Douglas McKellar had been a Senator from Tennessee since 1917 and had supported President Roosevelt in his election for President. Pitt Henslee was a large shareholder of First National Bank and was closely connected to Senator McKellar. Many in Dickson believed that First National was allowed to open because of those political connections.

144

The consequences of these actions for the citizens of Dickson included the curtailment of business, new layoffs and intensified suffering by those already hard hit.

B.C. was likely a depositor at the Citizens National Bank; otherwise, he would not have been at the meeting. He may have also been at the meeting representing the county's interest as Trustee. Nonetheless, it was a difficult time, and money was lost by many.

Dickson Furniture & Undertaking Company
L – R, Virginia Adcox, B. C. Nicks, Elmer Buckner, unknown, Clyde Fussell, unknown.
ca. 1940

In 1936 after he left the Trustee's office, B.C. went to work as a partner in the Dickson Furniture & Casket Company with Elmer Buckner and Clyde Fussell. This company was a stock company, owned by shareholders, much like Dickson Wholesale Grocery had been. Mr. Buckner and Mr. Fussell wanted to buy out all of the shareholders and turn the ownership of the store into a partnership. They solicited B.C.'s assistance in convincing the shareholders to sell because he was highly thought of in the community. In exchange, B.C. would become a partner. They were successful in this endeavor, and B.C. would remain there until his death in 1941.

After B.'s death, the partners would pay Kate $600 for her interest in the business. Sometime later Mr. Buckner and Clyde Fussell would dissolve the partnership. Mr. Fussell would retain the furniture business, naming it Dickson Furniture Store. Elmer Buckner would take the casket portion and begin Dickson Funeral Home.

On May 30, 1937, B.C. and Kate's oldest son, James, married Maxine Beard. Brother I. B. Bradley would perform the ceremony. The 1940 census shows that James and Maxine were renting a home on East College close to B.C. and Kate. On February 27, 1940, their first child, Judith Abigail, was born. This was the only grandchild that B.C. would ever know.

The 1940 census also shows B. and Kate living at 304 East College Street, with Bob, Carney and Lyle all living there. Bob's occupation is listed as the owner of a dry-cleaning business and he indicated that he had had 1 year of college. Carney and Lyle are listed as students with three years of college. It is not known if they were present for this survey or if the information was given by their parents. More than likely, they would have been at school. Carney graduated from U.T. in 1940, and Lyle graduated from Pepperdine in 1941.

In the late 1930s, B.C. had begun suffering from health problems associated with hypertension. By 1940 his condition had worsened, and he was under the care of a Nashville physician, a Dr. Bryan. In early 1941 Dr. Bryan suggested that B.C. and Kate go to Florida for a rest, in an effort to get his blood pressure under control. B.C. and Kate were close friends of Will Morrison Sr. and his wife, Tinnie, who had a place in South Miami, where they vacationed in the winter. They invited B.C. and Kate to come down and spend some time with them.

I have three letters that Kate wrote home during their stay that provide insight into B.C.'s condition at the time (Appendix G). The letters refer to other letters that were written home while they were in Florida, but these three are the only ones I know of that exist today.

I do not know specifically how long they stayed in Florida, but from the information provided in the letters they probably arrived around February 1, 1941, and stayed about 3 weeks.

Kate's first letter, dated February 4, was addressed to Carney, but the greeting addresses the boys—Carney, Bob and James. Lyle would have been away at school. In the letter, Kate expresses obvious concerns about B.C.'s condition. They had been to see a local physician referred to as Dr. Grimes. Kate stated that B.C.'s blood pressure at the initial visit was 250 over 150, 10 points higher than when they left home. This doctor assured them that he could help them, but they were both worried that he was just trying to "make some money off of us."

Kate describes B.C.'s condition as hypertension, and she states that B.C.'s feet were swollen. B.C. had expressed concern that his Nashville doctor, Dr. Bryan, had given up on him by sending them to Florida. It is obvious that they were both conflicted about what to do and in the letter ask the boys to get together and give them some advice.

Included in this letter is an additional note that Kate had written. She states in the appended note that she could not write the boys without B.C. wanting to read her every word and was therefore writing this additional note while he was asleep. She goes on to say B. had not written them because he was not feeling well enough to do so. She also reported that he had quit smoking, "he used to want to smoke bad," but that he now could no longer stand the smell of tobacco smoke. He apparently craved some things to eat, such as steak, fried oysters and cheese. She again asked the boys to write and tell them what they should do.

147

The second letter, dated February 10, was addressed to James at the Drug Store. She states that she had received letters from Max (Maxine) and Carney and was sorry to hear that Mr. Hayes had died. She also expressed shock over the news that "Miss Jessie" had had a stroke. She complained that the weather was cold and also that they were running short of cash, asking James to go to the bank and draw out $100 and to send it to them.

In this letter Kate states that B.C. was in the sixth day of his garlic treatment, previously prescribed by his Nashville physician, Dr. Bryan, and was feeling some better, though bothered by nausea. Kate says that Max had told her the "baby" (Abigail) was beginning to form words and would be walking soon.

The third letter is dated February 17 and is addressed to James. This letter was written to tell James to disregard a previous letter in which she had stated they were coming home the middle of the week. The weather had "turned pretty," and she was afraid that if they came home too early, B. would go back to work and suffer a setback. She also states that B. had continued with the treatment that he was taking when they left home. Kate indicated that James should not look for them until she called him from Nashville. This would indicate that they were traveling by train to and from Miami.

According to B.C.'s death certificate, he was admitted to Vanderbilt Hospital on February 27, 10 days after the third letter. If they did stay in Florida a little longer, his admission to the hospital could have occurred less than a week after they got home. B.C. would pass way at Vanderbilt Hospital on Wednesday, March 12, 1941, at 9:45 P.M., two days before his 60th birthday.

According to the death certificate, B.C. died from uremia complicated by malignant nephroscleosis. This would have meant kidney failure caused by chronic hypertension or high blood pressure. There was no treatment for this disease in 1940 and today would probably require dialysis. The death certificate is signed by

Dr. Randolph A. Cate. On March 17, the Monday following the funeral on Friday, Kate would receive the following letter from Dr. Thomas Frist Sr.

THOMAS F. FRIST, M.D.
208 Doctor's Building
NASHVILLE, TENNESSEE

Dear Mrs. Nicks

I was very sorry not to have seen you again after Mr. Nicks passed away. I believe you know how distressed that we were when we found that nothing constructive could be done for him. I am thankful that his last few days were peaceful. Even in the few days that I got to know him I grew very fond of him and could easily see why everyone speaks so very highly and kindly of him.

Each of you were lovely thru out his illness and I have never met a finer family. It is rare that even in sorrow that one has the many blessings that you have in the unusually fine sons & daughters-in-law. I would think that is the greatest blessing a mother could have. Even in the few days I knew Mr. Nicks, he was a real inspiration to me so it is easy to see where the boys get their finest with such a mother & father as they have.

Again, let me say I have thought of you often in your sorrow, and wished I could be of some comfort to you.

Kindly remember me to each of your splendid family.

I am sincerely yours,

Thos. F. Frist

There would be an outpouring of expressions of sympathy and tributes to the family over the next few days. His obituary, which ran in the Tennessean on Friday, March 14, 1941, reads as follows:

NICKS—At a Nashville infirmary Wednesday night at 8:30, B. C. Nicks, age 59 years. Survived by his wife, Mrs. Kate Lyle Nicks: four sons, Dr. James Nicks, Bob, Carney and Lyle Nicks, all of Dickson: four sisters, Mrs. E. W. Daniel of Dickson, Mrs. John Weems of Clarksville, Mrs. Dan Harris and Mrs. Robert Nicks of Nashville: four brothers, Emmett of Stayton, Tenn.: Speight of Memphis, Albert of Dickson and Dewey of Little Rock, Ark. The body will be at the Dickson Funeral Home until 2 P.M. Friday, will be carried to the Dickson Church of Christ for services conducted by Elder Leslie G. Thomas, assisted by Joe Larkins and Clay Pullias. Active pallbearers. Ovel Shelton, Dr. J. W. Beasley, Wesley McCord, Dr. S. M. Carter, Norman Fussell, William Daniel and James Corlew. Honorary. Officers of the Dickson Church of Christ, his business associates and close friends. Interment in Union Cemetery, Dickson, Tenn. Dickson Funeral Home, Dickson, Tenn., in charge.

Four Boys
B. C. and Kate Lyle Nicks
L-R Lyle, Carney, Bob & James

Chapter 11
The Last Word

Katherine Lyle Nicks, Abt 1959

On March 13, 1941, life without B. would begin for Kate. Soon she would experience the fear and anxiety of three of her boys leaving home to fight in World War II. James would be left behind and would become her rock during those difficult years.

She would live another 20 years and 11 months. She would see her boys become outstanding men with wonderful families. She would enjoy and love her four daughters-in-law. She would

152

live to see 11 of her 12 grandchildren born, as well as her first great grandchild. However, she did not have B.

She left us a wonderful treasure in the form of an annual diary, in which she would make entries on each anniversary of B.'s death. In this diary she wrote her own history of the last 21 years of her life. I include it here because it expresses perfectly the life that she and B. lived.

March 12, 1942

One year ago today, one who was very near and dear to me, passed from this world into the beyond. I have been deeply grieved and it has been a year of loneliness and great struggle for me.

Daily prayers for greater faith, strength and courage have helped me to be more resigned, and to carry on. I have been blessed in many ways—still have lots to be thankful for and shall always linger in the beautiful memories of him, his Christian life and his devotion to his family.

March 12, 1943

Another year has passed. I am still lonesome for him and miss him so very, very much. God has been good to me for which I am thankful. My prayer is to live true and faithful and have courage and strength to still carry on. God bless our boys in the service of their country and may they be brought back home safe and sound.

Three years ago today, and still, I am blue and lonely. I pray God daily for sufficient strength and unbounded courage, that I may face sorrows and tribulations, as I should.

March 12, 1945

Four years ago today the Heavenly Father saw fit to take from me my devoted companion. By the help of God I am carrying on the best I know how. A day never passes that I don't remember him and dwell on the happy memories of our life together. I pray the Lord that I may live the Christian life and be rewarded in the end.

March 12, 1946

Five years have come and gone. I still miss my loved one, but am more reconciled. I know it was God's will. His hand was in it all. I thank God that things are as well with me as they are. I am thankful my boys were all returned to me, safe and sound. I thank the Lord for all.

March 12, 1947

I am thinking today of one who was very dear to me. He was taken from me 6 years ago today. My life has been full of blessings. I thank God for my four fine boys, the wives and grandchildren. They all are so good to me and I love them all, but there is one vacancy that can never be filled. Heavenly Father, help

154

me in my lonely moments. May I live in that way that will be pleasing to thee and that will hold the love and respect of my children.

March 12, 1948

I've passed over another anniversary of B's death—7 long years. I know I have made a desperate effort to take my sorrow as my part in this life. I've kept my broken up feelings in my heart, and believe I can truly say that I haven't burdened my children. I pray for them daily that they may always live clean, upright, Christian lives. Help me, Lord, that I may live as thou woulds't have me.

March 12, 1949

Years come and go. Although I am constantly aware of the dark side of my life, in this date I am reminded, oh so forcibly, of the loss that has been mine. I have been unfortunate, in that my dear one left me, but there are those around me who are less fortunate than I. I pray for courage, faith and guidance. Especially do I pray for my children. May they always do the right things.

March 12, 1950

This is Sunday. I went to church and had a very lonely feeling. B. has been gone 9 yrs. today. Sometimes I wonder why I was left to walk alone, but I try to always say, "It was for the best, altho I may never know." Bob has just come by and said they were putting flowers on their Father's grave. I appreciate it so much. I

155

hope to live in a way that will be acceptable in God's sight. Lord help me, I pray.

March 12, 1951

I am passing over another anniversary of B's death. Ten years ago tonight. James, Bob and Carney each called me tonight. I appreciate their thoughtfulness. I am indeed fortunate to have a nice family. Lyle and Lucille live with me and are awfully sweet to me. I have tried hard to make the best of everything and hope that my children will always feel that I have done my best.

March 12, 1952

Eleven years ago today, both day of the week and day of the month, B. passed away. I am still doing my best to carry on, in every phase of life.

Mr. Alan Doty, one of B's best friends passed Sunday 9th just three days before B's death anniversary. I pray God daily that I can, with every endeavor live in accordance with His will.

March 12, 1953

This is B's death anniversary. Rufus McCaslin, cousin and close friend of B's was buried today. There are lots of memories that I can and do dwell upon. I thank God for my children, their wives and the grand-children. Everybody is nice and thoughtful of me. I am glad things are as well with me as they are. My prayers are for all, especially those who belong to me.

March 12, 1954

Thirteen years have passed since B's death. Things go on just about as they have since I've been alone. Thanks to my maker for all the good things of life and with his help, I will endeavor to carry on as best I can.

March 12, 1955

This is the 14th anniversary of B's death. I still have many things to be thankful for. Some days are long and dreary and I get so blue, but when I stop to count my blessing, I realize that I am truly blessed. God bless my boys, their sweet wives and the adorable grand-children. Help me, O God, to be worthy of all things that come my way.

March 12, 1956

Fifteen years ago today B. passed away in Vanderbilt Hospital. Seems such a long time. Had supper with Bob and Tunelle tonight. Had a hard time going to sleep. God bless my family and lead them all in the right paths.

March 12, 1957

Can it be possible another year has passed—16 years ago today, B. went away. For sixteen years I've walked alone. I've tried awfully hard to hold my chin up—to be brave and to be understanding. I thank God that things are as well with me as they are. I pray that I can constantly be aware of my blessings.

April 10, 1957

Fifty years ago today I was a Happy Bride.

March 12, 1958

Seventeen years ago, B. slipped away into the vast beyond. I miss him. I loved him. We were happy. But that is the way of life. Help me Lord to be understanding.

March 12, 1959 – Thursday

B. passed away 18 years ago today. I am thankful for my children, in-laws and grandchildren, and that things in general, are as well with me as they are.

March 12, 1960 – Saturday night

Have had a little depressed feeling today. B. has been gone 19 yrs. today. Heavenly Father, walk with me, and give me courage, faith, patience and Love.

March 12, 1961

Twenty years ago today. Such a long time to walk alone. I hope I have lived in a way that has been pleasing in God's sight. I pray that He, in his goodness, forgives the mistakes I make. I thank thee Lord for thy mercy.

Kate passed away on February 13, 1962, a month from the 21st anniversary of B.C.'s passing. The cause of her death was heart failure. Her funeral was held on Thursday, February 15, at the Walnut Street Church of Christ with E. Winston Burton conducting the service. Over 800 individuals attended the visitation, a testament to how highly she and her family were regarded in the community.

There are many ways a person may be measured, but the value of a spouse and their children are the best measures of a person's true significance on this earth. B.C. and Kate Nicks were Christians who loved each other and their family, were admired by friends and associates and were respected by all who knew them. We are so blessed to have come from "good stock."

"A good name is rather to be chosen than great riches, and loving favor rather than silver and gold" (Proverbs 22:1)

Appendix A
The Family of Absalom Doak Nicks Sr.

Born: March 6, 1794
Died: July 14, 1848
Married (1815): Hester Perry (10/8/1788–7/1858)

Children

- Perry Nicks (12/2/1816–abt. 1863) m. abt. 1838, Rebecca Davis
- Quinton Nicks (abt. 1818–8/14/1884) m. unknown, Elizabeth Walker Suffix (abt. 1820–abt. 1897)
- Allen Perry Nicks (12/9/1821–4/16/1910) m. 9/26/1841, Susan Rosanne Blocker
- Unknown daughter born abt. 1823
- Barton Warren Stone Nicks Sr. (7/24/1824–4/8/1894) m. 6/14/1847, America Agnes McGraw
- John H. Nicks (abt. 1825–abt. 1852) m. 8/15/1852, Elizabeth Jane Jones
- Absalom Doak Nicks Jr. (7/19/1826–1/24/194), m. 6/15/1845, Margaret Sophie Blocker
- Isaac H. Nicks (10/6/1827–7/6/1898) m. abt. 1867, Charlotte (Lottie) Baggett
- Unknown daughter born abt. 1829
- Robert Anderson Nicks (5/1830–11/12/1908) m. abt. 1870, Nancy Ann Puckett
- Stephen P. Nicks (2/15/1832–abt. 1901) m. 12/20/1853, Artemesia Warfield

Appendix B
The Family of Barton Warren Stone Nicks Sr.

Born: July 24, 1824

Died: April 8, 1894

Married (June 14, 1847): American Agnes McGraw (10/6/1831–3/19/1905)

Children

- Mary R. Nicks (11/8/1848–6/22/1903) m. 3/2/1869, John J. Hudgins
- Martha E. Nicks (3/6/1854–2/29/1936) m. 12/20/1866. Benjamin Tidwell McCaslin
- Henry Clay Nicks (3/6/1854–3/4/1928) m. 9/30/1875, Sophronia Rufus Matthews
- Caleb Newton Nicks (3/7/1856–10/13/0875)
- James Franklin Nicks (1/22/1858–9/28/1927) m. 12/24/1879, Eliza Harriett Bartee
- Eudora Ann Nicks (11/22/1859–3/19/1925) m. 4/30/1882) John M. (Jack) Speight
- Elenora W. Nicks (12/24/1861–5/4/1864)
- Barton Warren Stone Nicks, Jr. (6/25/1863–12/22/1935) m. 9/23/1897, Dottye Elinavent Phillips
- Florence A. Nicks (9/28/1865–2/23/1909) m. 10/30/1881, Elijah Washington Stark
- Stephen Ulisus Nicks (12/10/1867–1/7/1869)
- William Thomas Deloach–adopted (11/25/1877–12/3/1955) m. 12/31/1900, Josie Hayes
- Mary Ann Deloach–adopted (9/10/1880–unknown)

163

Appendix C
The Family of Henry Clay Nicks

Born: March 6, 1854

Died: March 4, 1928

Married (September 30, 1875): Sophronia Rufus Matthews (11/106/1857–4/6/1928)

Children

- Sara Agnes Nicks (9/18/1876–12/27/19540 m. 12/26/1901, Elijah Washington Daniel
- Lena Eudora Nicks (3/6/1879–9/28/1972) m. 4/16/1902, Robert Martin Nicks
- Buckner Clay Nicks (8/16/1881–3/12/1941) m. 4/10/1907, Martha Katherine Lyle
- Barton Rufus Nicks (10/13/1884–5/31/1904)
- Evie Jane Nicks (6/3/1887–7/23/1967) m. 10/10/1910, Daniel Heard Harris
- Charlie Emmett Nicks (8/12/1889–5/5/1962) m. 12/31/1914, Mary Palestine Larkins
- Jack Speight Nicks (10/4/1891–1/4/1980) m. 6/5/1924, Verda N. Talley
- Euvella Nicks (9/27/1894–6/7/1970) m. 9/10/1914, John Calvin Weems
- Anthony Albert Nicks (3/8/1897–6/17/1991) m. 4/15/1922, Lura Myrtice Fussell
- George Dewey Nicks (5/1/1899–9/23/1989) m. 8/18/1929, Hazel Edith Jones

Appendix D

Seven Letters from Elizabeth Lyle to Kate Nicks, 1909

What follows are transcripts and copies of seven letters written by my great-grandmother, Elizabeth Mabry Batson Lyle to her youngest daughter and my grandmother, Martha Katherine Lyle Nicks. These seven letters cover a period of time from March of 1909 until December of 1909.

Elizabeth Lyle was in her 65th year of life during this period, while Kate was 23. Kate was the youngest of eleven children and had married two years before on April 10, 1907. When the first letter was written, Kate was expecting her first child, James, who would be born on April 9, 1909. Kate was married to Buckner Clay ("B") Nicks, and during this time they made their home in Dull, Tennessee, in Dickson County. They shared a home with B's sister, Agnes, and her husband, Elijah Washington Daniel. Mr. Daniel and B were partners at that time in the mercantile business.

In a little over a month from the date of the last letter, Kate's father, William James Lyle, would pass away (February 10, 1910). Two months later (April 18, 2010) Elizabeth would also pass away. Much attention is given in the first letter to Kate's sister, Lizzie. Lizzie lived with her parents at the time and was 40 years old. She suffered all her life with an unknown affliction and would live until April 18, 1923, the thirteenth anniversary of her father's death.

These letters provide a remarkable insight into the last year of William James and Elizabeth Batson Lyle's life. Through these letters we are able to know something of the relationships they had with their children, grandchildren and neighbors. We learn something of the hardships they faced during this time and of their way of life. To have this kind of access into the day-to-day trials that our ancestors experienced over 100 years ago is unusual, even remarkable. I believe that Kate and her Mother would be pleased that their future family would still remember them and be interested in their lives.

Letter 1 — 3/4/1909

Dear Kate:

Will try to write you a little tonight, but hardly know what to say. The best news is that Lizzie getting on all right—seemingly. Poor thing has been through a terrible spell. I never saw anything like it in my life. Can't get over it—seem(?) She has been looking so well all the winter. I've been expecting something had to come. Has always been that way. Last Wed week ago we ironed & while she was ironing all at once she begun to shout & say the Lord had healed her of her afflictions & said she was going to die, but she got quiet & seemed all right, but a half past eleven that night woke me with a hard spell on her, then at half past four, had another, but got up that a.m. & went on until about eleven, when she had another while she was combing her hair. We put her to bed & she went on all night, until next day, had another, and one (?) about eleven got perfectly wild, so we had to chloroform her, & though she was kept under its influence, had spell after spell every ten minutes until dark, she got easy. I went to get supplies & after I got through cleaning up came in to find her in a dying condition. She lay on her back with eyes closed & never moved all night & her breathing could be heard all over the place. We were all sure she'd die before day light, but just at three she opened her eyes & was rational & has been ever since. Though she slept the whole time for three days and nights only when we'd speak to her. Guess it was the effects of chloroform. She has had two slight spells since. I was so in hopes that she would never have any more. She sat up three or four hours this p.m. & has a good appetite. Your aunt Sarah is staying with us & will stay until Lizzie seems well. Everybody has been mighty good to us. I hated mighty bad to telephone you, know it would excite you, but thought best to let you know at first. Am glad you didn't try to come, all the children

168

were here except you. Clay & Carney, Carney was suffering with his face, Matt came Sat night & stayed until Tues. A. & Lewis came Sun a.m. & A stayed until Mon. a.m. & Lewis went back Sun. Love, Effie nor Angie came. Had two such sweet letters from Effie. Had one from Bettie D. tonight. Said she thought of you while Lizzie was so bad off & was so sorry for you. Said she was going to write you soon. You don't know how hard this is on me. She told me time & again not to grieve one bit for her, for she was going to be at rest. But that night when I thought she was dying, I felt like I couldn't give her up at first, but at last became resigned to it, but would think how lonely I'd be here alone. It seems that she has been dead & resurrected. Don't know how long it will be before it will feel like the same place to me. Guess Sarah will stay with me another week. Wish I could see you, don don't know when that will be. Russell is here yet & will stay awhile longer. Don't know his future plans, Miss Ferrell is gradually going down. Guess Mrs Daniel is about in the same condition. Guess you did enjoy Annies visit. She talked like she had a nice time, too. Well, reckon I'll have to quit for this time. Will write again some time. When you write, don't say anything you wouldn't want Lizzie to see. She always reads my letters. Let me hear from you as soon as you can & tell me all about yourself. Accept best love for you both. Sarah & Lizzie send love to you also. Goodnight,

From your Mother

Letter 2 — 5/13/1909

Well Kate dear,

Will try to give you some news from our town. Guess you know of the death of Bailey Trotter. Poor Miss Emma is a sad widow again. Isn't it bad on her! You know she is in a family way.

I feel so sorry for her & Miss Bettie also. Think I never saw as large a crowd at a burial. He was buried by the IOOG Order after services held by Bro. Hill at the grave. His grave was concreted, so he is sealed up in side. Don't know what she will do, unless she goes back to Mr. Hudgins. It seems so strange to think he will never be seen around here again. A good many were down from Stayton, among the number B's mother & Aunt Jane. I spoke to both of them & invited them to stay with us, but they didn't. Mrs Nicks went by just now walking & I didn't know she was one her way home until she was past, & I didn't speak to her. Thought she would be back again, but Mrs Philips went on somewhere this a.m. (Clara's I reckon) & so Mrs. Nicks went on to go from there. Was sure she'd stop to see us awhile, I thought of going over to Mrs. Hudgins to see her, but thought maybe Miss Emma was there & wouldn't care for company. I went to see Carney on Monday & found him up & at his office. He is looking mighty bad. Has lost twenty lbs. Is going to Dawson this week. Dr. Felts thinks he will never get well unless he quits business for awhile & take a rest. I feel so uneasy about him. You know I am one that always looks on the dark side though.

Mrs. Hernden says when you come, she & Love are coming to spend a day with us. When are you going to come? I am so anxious to see you & little James, & B too. Is the baby still good? Tell him I have a little sucker for him when he comes. Hurry up & come, can hardly wait. Angie is planning a week with us right soon. Carney's children are coming again this summer, & Mary Corban is coming some time too. Bettie has been to see us twice about a minute each time. She is helping train the kids now for children's day which will be Sunday week. All the young folks are practicing for close of school too so our town is quite lively. Our missionary will have an all-day meeting 2nd Sunday in June. Saw Lizzie Willie yesterday. She says her sister Susie Herd is down with consumption & will be confined right soon. I think that is so sad. She, Mrs.

Neblett & a whole lot were asking about your son. Guess you knew Mary was gone. Had a letter from her today saying she hadn't been very well since she got home. H. Clay had just gotten over measles. All the rest were well. Also had a letter from Herman. He says he is coming here this fall. Hardly ever hear from Annie's. Mrs Hernden said she spent last Fri with them & said she would be in Nashville this week. I suppose to be at the closing exercises of Ward School. Her girls keep her in "a gallop & a trot," but they seem to enjoy it. How is your garden? Ours is looking fine so far. Have had onions, radishes, lettuce & mustard for some time. Wish you had some of our good old yellow butter. We can't use near all of it. I let Lila have a lot of it. Guess Lila will feel good when school closes. Annie has been sick for sometime & Louise at the store, so she had to get Jane Mckbee to stay with her. Mr Harper, Lois & Luna have all had a little spell this week, but are up now. Is Aunt Susan with you yet? Miss Reedie says she is nearly crazy to see you with a baby. They are fixed up mighty nice in the new home, and she seems very happy until she thinks perhaps she may get a germ. I never saw anyone so scary of catching diseases I think. They have re-papered & painted all the woodwork, floors & everything, & she is not going to use any rugs at all this summer. Well I guess I've told you enough nonsense for now. We are all as well as usual. Let me know when you are coming. With lots of love to you all,

Am as ever your loving,

Mother.

Well Kate: my darling child,

How are you standing this hot weather? Hope you and little James are getting on all right. Does he still have colic? You don't know how we did miss the sweet little thing. Every time I'd go in the room, couldn't help but look in the cot for him and the tears would come in spite of me. I'd give anything to see you all again. None of us are very well. Last week I helped to do the papering & just did get done by Sat eve after five days hard work. We made a real good job of it & it looks very nice. I was in bed the best part of Sun & Lizzie has been in bed two or three different times. Is sick today. Mr. Moore came this eve to go to painting. Don't know how long it will take him. It is so hard on us moving things around so much. We are expecting A. & F. Fri. & want to get fixed up before they come. Wish you all could be here. Lewis & family came on Sun after you left. Were so sorry they didn't get to see you. They have a right sweet little gang of boys. Angie is looking better than usual. Haven't seen Bettie since you left, except in passing. She went with Carney to town today. Mary is clerking for Bu??? & Louise is at ???? so Martha & Willie have the bag to hold. Martha telephoned me today to ask how you made jam & I really have forgotten, but told her how I thought it was. She asked a lot about you. Had a long sweet letter from Joanna last week. She asked me a whole lot about you. Said she could not realize that you were a little mother. Wants to see you so bad & expects to before summer is gone. Will be at home 1st July. Miss Emma is moving today over with Miss Stark. I do feel so sorry for her. I met her at the gate the other day & had a long talk with her. She is so resigned to her lot & talks so good about condition & everything. She will be confined in Oct. Mrs. Hudgins hasn't been very well for a week or more. Lila's folks are well & she & Louise are trying to paper some of

172

their rooms. Louise came in just now to see if Mr Moore wouldn't paper overhead for them. Said it nearly broke their necks & she didn't believe they could stand it. Haven't heard from Anne's lately except a card from Sarah. All well there. How did B's ice cream supper turn out? Wish I had me some right now. The Lewis company is still here & seem to have a big time going to the soda fount., playing croquet & driving. Mrs Hussey only stayed a week. She told Lila she would be so glad to see you. Said she thought so much of you. How is your garden? Ours is sinfully fine. Cabbage are all headed up, but it is too soon. They will rot before we can use them. Wilson Davis commenced yesterday to sow the orchard in peas, but didn't finish & hasn't done it today. He is also cutting off the pasture & we give him half the hay to save ours. I had to "catch all my hens & put them in pens" to keep them from eating the peas up. Expect the wheat thresher will be here soon. We have about 100 bushels (that is Chiles & us) half of it ours. We didn't have an interest in that on the ridge. It does seem so bad to see your Pa sitting around & taking no interest in anything. What Dr. can't attend to, have to telephone Carney to tell us. I do wish some of my own folks could come & live with us. Had the sweetest letter from Russell last week saying he felt like he ought to come and take care of us, but said he might be more expense than profit. I hate to ask any of you to come and take the responsibility of us on you, but it certainly would be a comfort to have some of you. If Dr. were to leave, don't know what we would do. I guess there will be some way provided for us. You know I'm so despondent anyway. It seems there is so little in life for me. But when I think of the trouble Carney has had & is still having & is so thoughtful of our welfare, I feel like I ought to be ashamed to complain at all. I know he is one of the best, most patient men in the world. Mr. Harper saw him yesterday & he seemed some better than usual. Well, tis most mail time so will close. Jane says tell you howdy &

kiss the baby for her. Let me hear from you real soon. With lots of love to you, B & baby, am as ever your

Affectionate

Mother

Letter 4 — 7/28/1909

Dear Kate:

I intended to write you when I sent the scraps(?) & tell you all about it, but didn't have time. I went to the store early Sat a.m. to get the goods & it was all gone, so I thought may be Miss Reedie had some & went to see her & got all she had, but she said she didn't need it & gave it to me without charge. I hope it was plenty. How are you all this hot day? We are in our usual health. Hope B is better than when you wrote. You all had better come down & stay a week or two with us. Can't you come Sat to the picnic? I can keep James at home & let you go. Whooping cough is in the neighborhood, but haven't heard of any except among the negroes. Ann's chaps have it & Reedie stopped her from washing for her. If I were you I'd not let those Daniel children come where the baby is. They surely wouldn't take exceptions at it. Don't suppose Mrs D. has ever thought about it & the children don't know. Even if they get mad, I think it's your duty to try to keep the baby from getting it. They say it is in a very bad form. Have heard of several deaths from it. So do your best to keep out of it. I want to see you all so bad. I know little James is sweet now. I hear from Minnie right-often. Says she has gained six lbs since she has been there. Had a letter from Mary the other day. Told me she had a mighty pretty diamond ring & said she supposed I understood it. She didn't tell who gave it but Louise said it was Sol Lewis, so guess she will soon be gone. Clay says they are having an awful drouth here. Everything burnt up. The old residents say it is the hottest & summer in 19 years. Clay has 34 head of hogs, some of them weigh 200 lbs, & it nearly works him to death to keep them watered & then it looks like some of them will die. Jewell made a fine crop & is at home now I guess until time to gather his crop. Clay says he wants to put them all in school this fall & wants Jewell to finish his education before he stops again. The young folks here have been having a fine time this summer visiting & having visitors. Louise & Lillian spent nearly two weeks at Springfield & Mary Merritt came home with them & stayed more than a week, left Monday. Think they had something to do nearly every night! Fred's mama entertained them last Sat night. Loyd Faires is at Lila's now for a two week stay. Annie came last Sat night-week and brought 4 children with her, left Angie & Sara & they are still here. They are lots of company for us. Are spending today at Lila's. Guess Mabel is in Nville now. She went to Carney's to stay one week & was to go from there to N. to stay two weeks. Guess Lucy will stay with us if she comes down here to school & maybe Bettie Corban & Lellie Harvey. Bettie D. & Bettie C are to teach in the public school I hear, & Prof H. & Louise will run the other school, with Irma as music teacher. I don't know whether these things are so or not, but is what I hear. Haven't seen Mrs Hudgins since you wrote but will try to find out & let you know when she is going. Guess you know Bouldin D. & Audrey Travis are married? What are Florence & Hilda doing with themselves? Guess they'll be down Sat. Give them my love, & tell them to make us a visit before school begins. A & F haven't been to see us yet. Angie said she wanted to come over this summer & stay long enough to go to see you & all the kinsfolk, but have no idea she can. I believe her baby is the prettiest one of the children. Matt told Dr. some time ago that he & Love were coming soon & stay two or three weeks, but you know it is easier to talk than act, & I don't expect them at all. Carney hasn't

175

been out since you were here, but am looking for him some time this week to straighten up ours & Chiles business. We made 108 bu. of wheat & one half of it is ours. Sold it yesterday the the mill for $1.05 per bu. I'm not canning any fruit at all. Have 16 can apples & 6 peaches left over from last year & preserves & jelly plenty, though will preserve some pears if they are any account. Haven't had but 3 gallons of berries brought me & I made 1 gal & a half of wine, would like to make more if I could get the berries. Have dried a few apples. Your Aunt Lizzie was down one day last week & we went to see Ann Harris. She is lots better. Sits up some. Lizzie said she was nearly crazy to see you & James. She said all the people up your way thought so much of you. Horace has gone back to N. to complete his business course & speaks of going to Okla to go in a banking business with Hugh McCauly (his mothers half Bro) John McC (Annie's Papa) is dying of cancer. I never have thought to tell you I got the darning thread all right & will settle with you when I see you. Eliza H came out again last week & I don't know whether she has gone back or not. She is "funny" again. Bettie hasn't been here since you were here & I haven't seen her often. She went to Monteagle & from there on to the place she taught & don't know whether she has gotten home or not. Miss Reedie is looking for Lucille this week to stay some with her. You asked about Russell. I hear from him real often & he thinks (one whole line faded out) & live with us. Says he will come & do the best he can for us, but thinks you & B are the proper ones to come. I'd be mighty glad to have some of you, but don't want any of you to make any sacrifice to please us. Well its nearly mail time so will close for this time. Write again soon & come Sat if you can. With lots of love to you all,

Am as ever your loving

Mother

September 2, 1909

Dear Kate:

Will try to write to write you a few lines this p.m. in answer to yours. Was glad to hear from you & to know you were getting along so nicely. I'm not at all well but stay up most of the time. Am so weak can hardly walk. Two weeks ago last Sun night had a hard nervous rigor which lasted an hour. Never had such a shake in my life. My jaws were almost locked. Haven't seen a well a day since the last day of July. I kind'a believe I've had a walking fever of some type. Nothing I eat agrees with me & my circulation is so bad. Hope to be better soon. Your Pa and Lizzie are about as usual. Annie, Jessie, Angie and Martha came last Sat night. They all went back Sun, except Jessie. She stayed until yesterday. Lucy & Mabel came last week & spent a day & night with us. Aunt Kittie Neblett came one morning & stayed a while before preaching. I was in bed & was so glad she came. I sometimes feel that I'm just dying of loneliness. Anyway, guess I'll have plenty company soon though, The Corban Girls are going to live upstairs & do light housekeeping during school. Bettie will be here in the morning & Joanna & Sarah & perhaps a Dunbar girl tomorrow p.m. Mary Corban is at Mt Eagle & Rev is going to Cumberland City to school Mon, & Mary will not return until Fri. So guess your Aunt Kittie will know how it feels for all the children to be gone. All the schools open Mon, so there will be quite a confusion for a few days. Lila is expecting several boarders & Sallie Scott will take some too. Marshall Hunter expected to take some, but he has typhoid fever, so don't expect he will yet, awhile. One of John Batson's boys has fever also. Harry Orgain has gotten about well, Lucy is preparing to go to Peabody. Maloy Lewis is going to C.Land city. Her father has bought a farm near there and will move xmas, I guess. I think Louise & Elizabeth Hunter are going to Wards. I may have told you all this before, I don't remember, Lucille Robertson went home today. Jessie & Angie spent a few days at Carney's last week & had a fine time. Carney & Mrs. H. carried them all out to the cave one night and stayed until a late hour. Carried their supper, consisting of barbecued pig, cake, ice cream & C. Heard from my ??? kids this week, all well, but nearly burnt out. Clay is figuring on selling out & leaving these. I'm afraid he will never be satisfied any more. Love left last week to spend sometime with her mother at Knoxville & then to Ashville N.C. for her health. Has been suffering intensely with hay fever this summer. Never hear from A. & F. nor Lewis & Angie. Huber was down last sun. He said A had quit Lyles & Blocks & gone into an incorporated firm, Wholesale auction (?) House. What are you doing these days? Don't wear yourself out saving fruit, I haven't made a thing except a doz glasses of apple jelly. Will make some pear preserves & sweet pickle if I ever get well enough. We are having the trees cut in the yard for stove wood. Two dead ones in front & two green ones in backyard at my window. We miss them lots. The sun comes in so hot. Have had a hand nearly two weeks getting wood. Have to pay him a dollar a day. It looks like it will take all we are worth to keep us going. Everything is so high. A dollars worth of bacon isn't much larger than my two hands & everything else in proportion. How is sweet little James getting along? Wish I could see you all. It seems if all of you were close enough for me to see oftener, I'd feel better. Mr. Hudgins told me yesterday he believes it was trouble that was making me sick. If trouble will do it, guess that is what is. I told Bettie D. how you were hurt at her not going to see you & she said she fully intended to do so, but kept going to other places until it was too late to go. Said she thought she'd get me to go with her, but I told her I couldn't go at all. Joanna asked her to go with her, but they don't know the way. I intended to go this fall & carry Lizzie but can't

178

leave your Pa, so you needn't expect us. Hope you can come again soon. Let me hear from you as often as you can. We all send lots of love to you all.

Lovingly your

Mother

Will inclose a letter from Minnie, so you may hear from them.

Letter 6 — 11/15/1909

Dear Kate:

I've been trying and trying to feel strong enough to write you for some time. So today am feeling better than I ever have & will scratch you a few lines. The picture of "little James" came this a. m., but I had planned to write you before it came. I think it is real good & it makes me want to see him so bad. Ten weeks ago today I was taken sick. It seems along old time to me. Mabel left me a week ago & I've been waiting on my self for a week. Get up at 5 o'clock, make a fire & go to my meals. Am taking nothing except Hamby's concentrated Dawson water & a striychminetoric. I feel like I could eat up the earth, but have to be a little careful yet. Don't swallow anything that I can't chew perfectly. Haven't tasted a biscuit since the day I was taken. Lizzie & your Pa are about as usual. We sold the hogs & calf & Carney has the horse, so your Pa doesn't have so much to run after. He isn't so much trouble only at night - Isn't blundering about so much. We have tried to get someone to come & stay with us so Dr. can get off, but have failed so far. The girls are still here, with the exception of Lellie. She went home yesterday to help nurse one of her half brothers at Lone Oak

179

who has typhoid fever. Don't' know whether she will come back or not. Joanna is busy with her program for xmas. Have you a Thanksgiving turkey? Haven't heard of anything to be done here except having the preacher. I think we are going to like him fine. He is a widower with six children, 5 girls and a boy, ranging from 2 to 13. Some of the Ladies met at Lila's last Thurs. to sew some for them. They held a church conference yesterday to straighten out the book & your name wasn't called, so guess you are all right. Guess you know Russell is traveling for a grocery firm in Okla. City. Had a card from him today & he said he was called the king coffee salesman of the city. Last week he sold 3600#. He has never told me what he is getting. Clay is selling groceries in Shamrock & likes it lots better than dry goods. I've had several sweet letters from Effie, but have never written her yet. Had a letter from A. last week saying there were coming soon if they could. Carney is so good to us, come real often to see after us. He is looking so well & I'm so glad to see him so lively. Lewis calls occasionally, but hardly ever hear from Matt & Love. Annie's folks are well & so are Lila's. She has only four boarders. Guess you know Lillian Scott is to marry xmas. They are going to have a big church wedding at the Methodist Church. They say Miss Emma has a mighty pretty sweet baby. I've never seen it. Annie Bell Williams has a son, born last Sat. Henry & Bettie Williams have another girl too. I've never seen Mattie Heard's baby yet. They say it is real pretty. If it is it doesn't favor the other one. You say you haven't a picture of your Pa & me so guess you can have the one that is here. I thought I gave each of you one. I don't know who has them all. Did you know Rufus had sold his home to Mr. McLaird and was coming back to the cabin? Think he aims to build soon. Miss R says she wants to come back home. I don't see her very often. Miss Rosa was to see me not long ago. Most of the neighbors have been very good to come to see me. Eliza Harris has sent for Jane to go & stay with her. I don't think they have treated me right at all. Wrote to Jane

180

& never said a word to me about it. I told your Aunt Martha the other day I didn't know whether I was going to give my consent for her to go or not. I'll have to get some one else if I do & it isn't a very easy task to get one. I'd rather do the work myself, but don't believe I'll be strong enough soon. Bettie comes sometimes & always asks about you. Told me to make haste & get well & go with her to see you. Wish we could. The pretty weather we've had made me want to go to see you so bad. I'm nearly crazy to see you all. When can you come ? Wish you didn't live so far from us. What are Florence & Hilda doing? Give them my kindest regards & also their mother. Well my sides & back are so tired will have to stop. Let me hear from you soon & come as soon as you can. Kiss that sweet old baby right in the mouth for me. With lots & lots of love from all to you all, am as ever

Your own mother

Letter 7 — 12/26/1909

Dear Kate:

Have been wanting to write you for some time but am feeling so bad, don't feel like doing anything. Your Pa, Lizzie & I have been all by ourselves all xmas, & it is so lonesome & sad. Haven't seen any of the children except Lila. She is so good, comes every day to see after us & nearly always brings something good to us. Your Pa has been a lot of trouble since Sun., until today. Is better? He takes a notion he's out at home, & runs off & I'm not able to run after him, so I have to depend on the kindness of anybody. Hubert has been staying with us at night. & Looks after your Pa during the day. Day before yesterday he went to the creek, & when he got back, was perfectly exhausted & fell in the floor. I think he misses Dr. I'm not getting on well at all, am so weak can

181

hardly get up stairs. My stomach is sick all the time, & any bowels are so swollen can't half get about. Jane has been gone to Eliza's a week, & we are just living from hand to mouth. I manage to cook a little breakfast & then we warm up things in the reflector & sit around the fire to eat. I may get Lydia after xmas. I spoke to Dump Hagwood this a.m. about Mattie Hodges living with us & he spoke as thought he thought she would. I'd so much rather have a nice white girl & the negroes charge so much. There is so little to be done here. I feel like it is perfectly awful to pay $2.00 a week & then they waste & steal so much. Carney aimed to come today but was so cold, backed out. He called just now & asked if we were warm & comfortable. Bless his dear heart. He is so thoughtful of us. Miss Hernden called the other day & told us to bundle up & go over there & stay a while, but La' me we can't go anywhere. Lilian's marriage takes place tonight. They will have a cold affair. Mabel expected to come & we kinda looked for Annie too, but Mabel called just now & said they wouldn't come. Bro. Powers is holding protracted services, day & night during xmas. Said he thought maybe it would cut out so much partying. It has been a very quiet xmas so far, I haven't sent a present or even a card, but have gotten several. Carney gave me a stand of lard, Lila a cake & some pies. The girls upstairs a box of fruit & nuts, also a can each of oysters, salmon & vienna sausage. Miss Mary Caldwell a nice book. A. & F. a kimona for me, a jacket for Lizzie, also one for you. Florence sent your Pa a neck warmer, Mary Lyle a pie for me & a chamis for toilet powder. Clay, M & the boys a big box of nuts & fruit & a quarter of a big fruit cake. Miss Matt Dunn a sack of sausage. Matt & Love a mighty pretty centre piece for me & a jacket and prim to Lizzie. Love is so sad. She wrote me & told me she missed her sister more & more, especially at xmas & her mother is giving up. I know she does feel bad. Said Matt had been suffering with neuralgia some. I do hope he'll not have such a time as Carney. Love said James was the sweetest baby she ever saw and she wanted to take him away from you. Miss Herndon told me one day over the phone that she knew he was the prettiest, sweetest & best baby in the world, & she enjoyed your visit so much. Lewis called last night & said he thought of us & wanted to send us something, but was so busy. Haven't even had a card from Russell. I forgot to tell you that this a.m. Mrs. McCommee sent me a plate of butter & some stuffed sausage. You know we sold our cow & haven't had to buy milk nor butter either since. After the store was burned we were turned out of doors here & couldn't keep the cow with out lots of trouble & its so expensive to keep a cow. What we'd pay for bran would buy all the milk & butter we need, besides the trouble of milking & churning. Mr. Harper is kept busy marrying people. 23, he married. Mattie Bagwell, Sun. night, Neal _____ & Mannie Adeshold, tonight. Lilian & Orville yesterday eve. Andrew James & a Forsythe girl came out there, went in & were married. Louise played the march for them. A week or so ago a Hagwood boy & Hollis girl came to the gate & had the knot tied. It seems the harder the times, the more they marry. Mr. Ferrell was here yesterday & told me that Miss F's sister who married about two yrs ago has left her husband & gone back to her father's. Cause, dissification [disaffection? I think you may need a bracketed "sic" here] & neglect. Well, xmas will soon be gone & I'll not be sorry. Guess the Corban girls will be back Fri., then we won't be so lonely. Lillie will not come any more I guess. We had xmas cards from Miss Sara Winn & she sent best love to you. Haven't seen any of your Aunt Martha's folks at all. Guess they are out with us. Will tell you when I see you. Perhaps you got a hint while you were at Carney's. I'm just dying for some of you to come & be with us some, but can't blame you while it is so cold. Hubert says he'd like very much to see you & Minnie told me in her last letter to tell you that she appreciated James' pictures & she was going to write you soon. Well, I'm getting tired so will close. You & B accept our dearest love and kiss James until you get tired for me. Come just as soon as you can & write me often. You don't know how glad it makes me to get even a card. Byby for this time. Wishing you a Happy New Year.

Am as ever your, Mother

(added at the top of page 1):

Many, many thanks to you for remembering me Xmas. I haven't made a single present - am ashamed to say, but you know the reason. By-By Lizzie.

Appendix E
Prices of Merchandise in 1930s
Nicks Brothers General Merchandise Store
Wrigley, Tennessee

Clock - $1.05

Bulb - $.10

Coffee - $.55

Prunes - $.35

Peas - $.35

Onions - $.15

Soda - $.25

Coconut - $.10

Soap - $.25

Marshmallows - $.10

Sweater - $2.65

Hominy - $.25

Print - $.40

Meat - $.25

Salt - $.05

Crax - $.20

2 Shirts - $2.35

2 underwear - $1.00

3½ yds. Print - $.70

Pineapple - $.20

Bananas - $.10

Oysters - $.25

3½ yds. seersucker - $1.23

Appendix F

Official Vote in Dickson County for Trustee – 1930

Box	1	2	3	4	4	5	5	6	6	7
Precinct	Garner's Creek	Pomona	Abiff	Burns	Brown's Chapel	Dickson 1	Dickson 2	Charlotte	Sylvia	White Oak Flats
Hunt	73	59	75	87	47	365	184	95	46	59
Nicks	43	44	36	92	21	226	143	224	55	55
Phillips	18	13	20	12	15	66	46	103	23	33

Box	8	8	9	9	10	11	12	13	14	15	
Precinct	Cumberland Furn.	Stayton	Vanleer	Slayden	North Yellow Ck	Ruskin	White Bluff	Tenn City	Claylick	Dull	TOTALS
Hunt	62	46	26	40	32	122	86	51	6	35	1596
Nicks	114	41	74	54	57	99	176	20	37	97	1708
Phillips	70	33	43	29	10	15	20	11	3	49	632

Appendix G
Three Letters to Home from Kate — 1941

First letter — 2/4/1941

Kate Nicks
South Miami, Florida
Tuesday, February 4, 1941, 12:45 P.M.
To: Carney Nicks
Dickson, Tennessee

Dearest boys, Carney, Bob & James —

B. went to see the doctor here this a.m. [Dr. D. H. Grimes] who has an office here in So. Miami and a clinic in Coral Gables. He found B.'s blood pressure 250 over 150 which is 10 points higher than it was when he left home. Of course he does not know what is causing this hypertension, but says something is and says he is the kind to not give up until he tries. Said he had never had a case that he couldn't do something with and believes in trying to find the cause. Of course we don't know whether he is just trying to make some money off of us or what. But he has been recommended here as an awfully good doctor. Father said he wishes he could see you boys and let you advise him what to do. Of course he might spend a lot of money with him trying to locate his trouble and finally find it, which would be grand. Then again, it might not do any good. He made a "urinalysis" this morning but that will not be reported on until tonight when he has to go back to the office. He asked Father if his ankles swell and of course we know they do.

Father seems to think that Dr. Bryan sent him off down here to rest and that nothing more could be done, while this doctor down here seems to want to try to do something to find the cause of high blood pressure, which in a way sounds interesting to us and on the other hand, as I said might mean a chance for him to make some money. You boys talk this over and write us as soon as you can. What would you advise?

It rained here yesterday and the air is much cooler today. Father was so cool, that when we started out for a drive this a.m., he wore his overcoat and seemed perfectly comfortable, and I wore my coat. We took a nice drive over some roads we had never been over before. We see lots of pretty flowers, shrubbery, etc. Carney, there are oodles of poinsettias (like the flowers you gave Sister and Maxine last year) growing from 1 ft. to 8 & 9 ft. high. I think they are beautiful.

James wrote us you had been to Nville to see Mr. Inge — you might write us just what you all agreed upon. I believe I have nothing more to write, now, but will write again tomorrow.

Had a card from Verda Saturday saying Hazell's father did pass away. I wrote Hazell a letter this p.m.

Love to all — Mother

[Kate added the following text to the foregoing letter.]

Boys-

I haven't been able to write you all a word since I've been here that he couldn't see — He has sat right by me when I write and reads every page as fast as I finish it. He is awfully blue today since he went to the doctor. I asked him if he wanted to write you all himself, and he said he simply couldn't do it. He is so nervous or something that he hasn't written to anyone except two or three

190

cards and you could hardly read them. He is asleep now and I'm slipping this little extra page in, so he won't know it. He is getting rest, nothing but rest, eating well and everything is just as pleasant as can be. Doesn't have a thing to worry about. He told me today that he kind of believes Dr. Grimes thinks it might be due to prostatic trouble. I don't want him to know I am telling you that. We don't know what to do about letting this doctor take home in hand. He has changed in some respects since he came down here. Use to want to smoke bad and now can hardly stand to smell tobacco smoke and doesn't want to smoke himself. He gets to craving some things to eat. Came in the other day with a big steak to cook, craved fried oysters for several days, so he and Will bought some and Tennie fried them, also craves cheese and has bought some twice. Write us right away what you think we should do. We drove quite a bit this a.m. but Father didn't seem to enjoy it like he usually does, which makes me know he is worried about himself.

Second Letter — 2/10/1941

Kate Nicks
South Miami, Florida
Monday, February 10, 1941, 1:00 P.M.
To: James Nicks
Dickson, Tennessee

Dear James —

This morning we received Maxine and Carney's letters telling of Mr. Hayes death and Miss Jessie's illness. Was so sorry to hear of both cases, but was expecting to hear of Mr. Hayes death. Was shocked to learn of Miss Jessie's condition and do wish I knew

191

more about it. Is she conscious? And do they think she will get over this stroke?

It is real cold her today. Don't you folks get it into your heads that it is so warm and comfortable here. The thermometer this a.m. was 42 degrees. The sun is shining and when you are in it away from the wind it feels good and warm, but the wind without the sun is real cold. Father is wearing his overcoat today. An old man here this morning said it had been the coldest all around winter that they had known for years. We had a beautiful day Saturday and Mr. Morrison just raved over it, but then he came to the conclusion last night and today that it is uncomfortably cold. You see, we can't have fires. Where we are staying is a fireplace, but wood is scarce and we just have a sprinkle of fire — helps some though.

James, Father wants you to go to the bank and get four $25.00 Cashier checks and mail them to him. We are about to run low in money. Send them right away. Father is in the 6th day of his 10 day garlic treatment. He feels better today than he did yesterday — is bothered so much with nausea and I think it is when he begins to get hungry, for when he eats he gets better.

Tell Max I will answer her letter soon — she says the baby is beginning to say some words and is about to walk. Must close and get this in our mail.

Love to all —

Mother

Third Letter — 2/16/1941

Kate Nicks
South Miami, Florida
Sunday, February 16, 1941, 2:30 P.M.

To: James Nicks
Dickson, Tennessee

Dear James —

Since writing you yesterday that we planned to go home the middle of this week, the weather is pretty here and Father is feeling some better, so we plan to stay some longer, if the sun keeps shinning. In other words, don't' look for us until we call you from Nashville.

On second thought, he would not be able to go to work if we were there and he might try to do it and have a real backset. He has gone back to the treatment he was on when he left home and think he is going to feel better.

We have seen about all of the southern part of Florida we care to see, but if we get a chance, would like to see some of the central part and the West Coast. He was not able to go to Key West with the Morrisions, but don't think we missed so very much.

Haven't much to write this time, just wanted to follow up yesterday's with this change of mind.

Love,

Mother

Notes

[1] James G. Leyburn, *The Scotch-Irish: A Social History* (Chapel Hill: University of North Carolina Press, 1962), p. 180.

[2] Ibid, p. 327.

[3] Ibid, p. 180.

[4] S. M. Rankin, *History of the Buffalo Presbyterian Church and Her People* (Jos. J. Stone & Co., Greensboro, N.C.: 1934), p. 10.

[5] Ibid., p. 16.

[6] Ibid., p. 11.

[7] E. W. Caruthers, *A Sketch of the Life and Character of the Rev. David Caldwell, D.D.* (Greensboro, N.C.: Swain & Sherwood, 1842), p. 24.

[8] Ibid., p. 14.

[9] Rankin, *Buffalo Church*, p. 26

[10] Ibid., p. 27.

[11] Sallie W. Stockard, *The History of Guilford County, North Carolina* (Knoxville, Tennessee: Gaut-Ogden Co., 1902), pp. 12- 15.

[12] Rankin, *Buffalo Church*, pp. 19-20.

[13] Lawrence E. Babits and Joshua B. Howard, *Long, Obstinate and Bloody: The Battle of Guilford Courthouse* (Chapel Hill: The University of North Carolina Press, 2009), p. 122.

[14] Rankin, *Buffalo Church.*, p. 189

[15] Ibid., p. 199.

[16] *The Goodspeed History of Dickson County, Tennessee* (The Goodspeed Publishing Company, 1886) pp. 56-57

[17] "The Nashville Road," htpp://freepages.genealogy.rootsweb.ancestry.com. Last modified March 1, 2013.

[18] *Goodspeed*, p. 56-57.

[19] W. Jerome D. Spence and David L. Spence, *Spence's History of Hickman County, Tennessee,* (np.,1900) p. 63.

[20] *Goodspeed*, p. 56

[21] Rubel Shelly, *I Just Want to Be a Christian* (Nashville: 20th Century Christian, 1984).

[22] J. D. Murch, *Christians Only* (Eugene, Oregon: Wipf & Stock, 2004), p. 360.

[23] Leroy Garrett, *The Stone-Campbell Movement: The Story of the American Restoration Movement* (Joplin, Missouri: College Press Publishing Company, 2002), p. 71.

[24] *Goodspeed*, p. 56-57

[25] Ibid.

[26] Ibid., p. 57

[27] Ibid., p. 57

[28] Ibid., p. 57

[29] Ibid., p. 57

[30] Earl Schmittou, Jr., "Bicentennial Flashback, Stayton Beginnings," *Dickson Free Press* (March 25, 1972), p. 11.

[31] Ibid., p. 11.

[32] *Goodspeed*, p. 57

[33] *Wikipedia*, s.v. "Henry Clay," last modified June 19, 2015, http://en.wikipedia.org/wiki/Henry_Clay.

[34] *Wikipedia*, s.v. "Whig Party (United States)," updated June 19, 2015, http://en.wikipedia.org/wiki/Whig_Party_(United_States).

[35] Tolbert Fanning, "Duty of Christians in Reference to the Political Crisis of 1861" *The Gospel Advocate* 2 (1861), no. 2: 35.

[36] Ibid., pp. 35-36.

[37] Spence, *History of Hickman County*, p. 159.

[38] Spence, *History of Hickman County*, p. 142.

[39] Frank H. Smith, *The History of Maury County*, (Maury County Historical Society, 1969), p. 48.

[40] Ibid., p. 48.

[41] Spence, *History of Hickman County*, p. 160.

[42] Ibid., p. 160.

[43] George Jackson, "Cumberland Furnace, A Frontier Industrial Village," in *The Tennessee Encyclopedia of History and Culture*, University of Tennessee, 1994, http://www.tennesseeencylopedia.net/entry.php?rec=337, (Retrieved August 15, 2016).

[44] *Goodspeed*, p. 57.

[45] *Goodspeed*, p. 62.

[46] Schmittou, "Stayton Beginnings," p. 11.

[47] Ibid., p. 11.

[48] *Goodspeed*, p. 62.

[49] Dickson County Court Records, Minute Book 1800-1886, p. 456

[50] Edward L Ayers, *Southern Crossing, A History of the American South, 1877-1906*, (New York: Oxford University Press, 1998), p. 5.

[51] Ibid., p. 45.

52 Schmittou, "Stayton Beginnings," p. 11.

53 Ibid.

54 Capt. A. A. Matthews, Obituary, *Nashville Tennessean*, April 24, 1912, p. 1.

55 Anthony A. Matthews, Obituary, *Nashville Banner*, April 27, 1912, p. 1.

56 Schmittou, "Stayton Beginnings," p. 11.

57 Ibid.

58 Schmittou, "Stayton Beginnings," p. 11.

59 United States v. American Tobacco Co., 221 U.S. 106 (1911)

60 Schmittou, "Stayton Beginnings," p. 11.

61 Mrs. R. M. Workman, "Southside, Tennessee, Schools," http://www.tngenweb.org/ montgomery/hissouthside.html, (Retrieved June 16, 2016).

62 Ibid.

63 Louise Littleton Davis, "The First Seventy Five – A History of The First National Bank of Dickson" (a private publication, July 21, 1978), p. 84.

64 Eddie Williams Swank, "Walnut Street Church of Christ, 1891-1953" (A private paper written about 1954).

65 . Schmittou, "Stayton Beginnings," p. 11.

66 Frederick Lewis Allen, *The Big Change – America's Transformation 1900-1950* (New York: Harper and Row, 1952). eBook No. 0500881h.html (2005). Ch. 2 Part II.

67 Carhistory4u.com –History of the Motor Car/Automobile Production 1900-2003, http//:www.carhistory4u.com/the-last-100-years/car-production. (Retrieved August 21, 2016).

68 · Encyclopedia Britannica Online, s.v. "Rural Free Delivery," updated 1998, http//:www.britannica.com/ruralfreedelivery. (Retrieved June 6, 2016).

69 Raghruam Rajan and Rodney Ramcharan, "The Anatomy of a Credit Crisis: The Boom and Bust in Farm Land Prices in the United States in the 1920s," *The Federal Reserve Board, Finance and Economics Discussion Series,* May 30, 2012, p. 1.

70 "Dickson Business Leader is Dead," *Tennessean* (Nashville, Tennessee), March 13, 1941, p. 16. (Retrieved from https://www.newspapers.com/image/148001043).

71 "Dickson," October 28, 1923, *Tennessean* (Nashville, Tennessee), p. 37. (Retrieved from https://www.newspapers.com/image/178352356).

72 Dickson County Register's Office, Deed Book 58, p. 227.

73 "Trustee B. C. Nicks Residence Burglarized," *Dickson Herald* (Dickson, Tennessee) November 11, 1930, p. 1.

74 Dan Bryan, "The 1933 Banking Crisis—from Detroit's Collapse to Roosevelt's Bank Holiday" *American History USA,* http://www.americanhistoryusa.com/1933-banking-crisis-detroit-collapse-roosevelt-bank-holiday/, (Retrieved February 8, 2017).

75 Robert Jabaily, "Bank Holiday of 1933," *Federal Reserve History.* https://www.federalreservehistory.org/essays/bank-holiday-of-1933 (Retrieved February 8, 2017).

76 Davis, *"First National Bank,"* p. 48.

CPSIA information can be obtained
at www.ICGtesting.com
Printed in the USA
BVOW08*1952181017
498048BV00002B/58/P